Greg Byrd, Lynn Byrd and Chris Pearce

Cambridge Checkpoint
Mathematics

Skills Builder Workbook

8

CAMBRIDGE
UNIVERSITY PRESS

CAMBRIDGE
UNIVERSITY PRESS

University Printing House, Cambridge CB2 8BS, United Kingdom

One Liberty Plaza, 20th Floor, New York, NY 10006, USA

477 Williamstown Road, Port Melbourne, VIC 3207, Australia

314–321, 3rd Floor, Plot 3, Splendor Forum, Jasola District Centre, New Delhi – 110025, India

79 Anson Road, #06–04/06, Singapore 079906

Cambridge University Press is part of the University of Cambridge.

It furthers the University's mission by disseminating knowledge in the pursuit of education, learning and research at the highest international levels of excellence.

www.cambridge.org
Information on this title: www.cambridge.org /9781316637395 (Paperback)

First published 2017

20 19 18 17 16 15 14 13 12 11 10 9

Printed in Great Britain by CPI Group (UK) Ltd, Croydon CR0 4YY

A catalogue record for this publication is available from the British Library

ISBN 978-1-316-63739-5 Paperback

....

Contents

Introduction

Welcome to Cambridge Checkpoint Mathematics Skills Builder Workbook 8

The *Cambridge Checkpoint Mathematics* course covers the Cambridge Secondary 1 Mathematics curriculum framework. The course is divided into three stages: 7, 8 and 9.

You can use this Skills Builder Workbook with Coursebook 8 and Practice Book 8. It gives you extra practice in all the topics, focusing on those that are the most important, to improve your understanding and confidence.

Like the Coursebook and the Practice Book, this Workbook is divided into 18 units. In each unit there are exercises on each topic. There are introductory explanations and either worked examples or guided questions. These explain the skills you need to master and use to solve more complex problems. This Workbook also gives you a chance to try further questions on your own. This will improve your understanding of the units. It will also help you to feel confident about working on your own when there is no teacher to help you. At the end of each unit is a link to exercises to attempt in the Coursebook.

If you get stuck with a task:

- Read the question again.

- Look back at the introductory explanations and worked examples or guided questions.

- Read through the matching section in the Coursebook.

1 Integers, powers and roots

1.1 Integers

Integers are whole numbers.

They can be positive like these: 2, 17, 543

They can be negative like these: −3, −28, −921

You need to be able to add integers. For example:

$3 + {-5} = -2$ $-6 + {-3} = -9$ $-5 + 7 = 2$

A number line can help you:

> Think of $3 + {-5}$ as $3 − 5$.

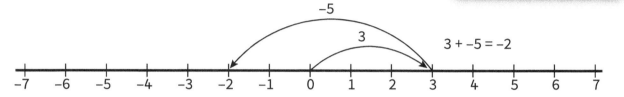

1   Complete these additions.

a $-2 + {-5} = \ldots\ldots$

b $5 + {-7} = \ldots\ldots$

c $-4 + 4 = \ldots\ldots$

d $-2 + 8 = \ldots\ldots$

2   Draw a line from the addition to the answer. The first one has been done for you.

3 + 1

−6 + 2   4

6 + −2

−3 + 7   −4

−2 + −2

−6 + 2

3 Fill in the missing numbers.

The answer is always 1.

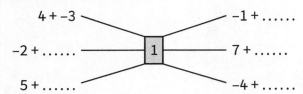

Here are some examples of subtracting a positive number:

$4 - 3 = 1$ $4 - 5 = -1$ $-2 - 5 = -7$ $-6 - 1 = -7$

4 Complete these subtractions.

a $4 - 6 = \ldots\ldots$ **b** $2 - 4 = \ldots\ldots$ **c** $-1 - 2 = \ldots\ldots$ **d** $-2 - 3 = \ldots\ldots$

e $8 - 3 = \ldots\ldots$ **f** $3 - 8 = \ldots\ldots$ **g** $-4 - 4 = \ldots\ldots$ **h** $-3 - 6 = \ldots\ldots$

To subtract a negative integer, change it to an addition of a positive number:

Change − −2 to + 2.
Change − −5 to + 5.

$3 - -2 = 3 + \mathbf{2} = 5$ $3 - -5 = 3 + \mathbf{5} = 8$ $-3 - -4 = -3 + \mathbf{4} = 2$

5 Complete these subtractions.

a $2 - -5 = 2 + 5 = \ldots\ldots$ **b** $-3 - -2 = -3 + \ldots\ldots = \ldots\ldots$

c $1 - -4 = 1 + \ldots\ldots = \ldots\ldots$ **d** $-5 - -6 = -5 + \ldots\ldots = \ldots\ldots$

6 Fill in the missing numbers.

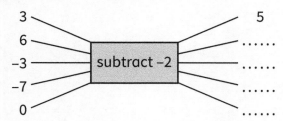

Here is a rule for multiplication:

Same signs, positive answer

$3 \times 4 = 12$

$-3 \times -4 = 12$

Different signs, negative answer

$-3 \times 4 = -12$

$3 \times -4 = -12$

7 Complete these multiplications.

a 2 × –5 = ...   **b** –2 × –5 = ...   **c** –2 × 5 = ...

8 Complete these multiplications.

a –6 × 3 = ...   **b** 5 × –5 = ...   **c** –7 × –3 = ...

9 Complete these multiplications.

a 10 × –4 = ...   **b** –6 × –7 = ...   **c** –9 × 6 = ...

10 Complete these multiplication tables.

×	3	–4	–5
–2	–6		
–3			15
4			

×	–6	–1	7
4			
–5			
–8			–56

11 Fill in the missing numbers.

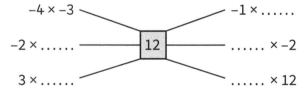

The answer is always 12.

12 Fill in the missing numbers.

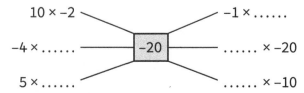

The answer is always –20.

Now try Exercise 1.1 on page 9 of Coursebook 8.

1.2 Prime numbers

Look at this table, which shows **factors** of some numbers.

Number	Factors
6	1, 2, 3, 6
7	1, 7
8	1, 2, 4, 8
9	1, 3, 9

You can divide 6 by 1, 2, 3 or 6 without a remainder.

7 only has TWO factors. 7 is a **prime number**.

Is 15 a prime number?

15 = 3 × 5.   3 and 5 are factors of 15.   15 is NOT a prime number.

1 Circle the prime numbers.

2   3   4   5   6   7   8   9   10

2 Circle the prime numbers.

11   12   13   14   15   16   17   18   19   20

3 Complete these lists of factors.

a Factors of 12:   1   2   3   12

b Factors of 16:   1   2   16

c Factors of 24:   1   2   3   4   24

d Factors of 20:   1   2   20

e Factors of 21:   1   21

4 Look at the answers to Question 3.

Write down the HIGHEST number that is a factor of both 16 and 24.   ......

This is the **highest common factor (HCF)** of 16 and 24.

5 Find the HCF of 16 and 20. ......

6 Find the HCF of 12 and 24. ......

7 Find the HCF of 12 and 21. ......

Look at the lists below. The lowest number to appear in BOTH lists is 10. **The lowest common multiple** (LCM) of 2 and 5 is 10.

Multiples of 2:   2   4   6   8   10   12   14   16   18   20

Multiples of 5:   5   10   15   20   25   30   35   40   45   50

8 **a** Fill in the gaps in the list of multiples of 3.

   3   6   9   15   21   30

b Find the LCM of 3 and 2 ......

c Find the LCM of 3 and 5 ......

9 **a** Fill in the gaps in the lists of multiples.

Multiples of 4:   4   8   16   24   32   40

Multiples of 6:   6   18   24   36   48   54   ......

b Find the LCM of 4 and 6 ....

c Find the LCM of 4 and 5 ....

d Find the LCM of 5 and 6 ....

You can use a table like this to find prime numbers.

1	2	3	4	5	6	7	8	9	10
11	12	13	14	15	16	17	18	19	20
21	22	23	24	25	26	27	28	29	30
31	32	33	34	35	36	37	38	39	40
41	42	43	44	45	46	47	48	49	50

Cross out number 1.

Draw a circle round number 2. Cross out all the multiples of 2.

> Cross out 2, 4, 6, ...

Draw a circle round number 3. Cross out all the multiples of 3.

> Some are already crossed out. Cross out 9, 15, ...

Draw a circle round number 5. Cross out all the multiples of 5.

Draw a circle round number 7. Cross out all the multiples of 7.

10 Draw a circle round all the remaining numbers. List them below.

. . . .

These are the prime numbers less than 50.

Now try Exercise 1.2 on page 12 of Coursebook 8.

2 Sequences, expressions and formulae

2.1 Generating sequences

Here is a sequence of numbers: 2, 4, 6, 8, 10, ...

The first term of the sequence is 2.

The **term-to-term rule** is 'Add 2'.

> You add 2 to each number to get the next number:
> 2 + 2 = 4, 4 + 2 = 6, 6 + 2 = 8, etc.

---

1 Write down the first five terms of each sequence.
Some have been started for you.

a First term: 1   term-to-term rule: 'Add 2'

$$1 \overset{+2}{\longrightarrow} 3 \overset{+2}{\longrightarrow} 5 \overset{+2}{\longrightarrow} \ldots \overset{+2}{\longrightarrow} \ldots$$

b First term: 10   term-to-term rule: 'Add 3'

$$10 \overset{+3}{\longrightarrow} 13 \overset{+3}{\longrightarrow} 16 \overset{+3}{\longrightarrow} \ldots \overset{+3}{\longrightarrow} \ldots$$

c First term: 9   term-to-term rule: 'Subtract 1'

$$9 \overset{-1}{\longrightarrow} 8 \overset{-1}{\longrightarrow} \ldots \overset{-1}{\longrightarrow} \ldots \overset{-1}{\longrightarrow} \ldots$$

d First term: 20   term-to-term rule: 'Subtract 2'

$$\ldots \overset{-2}{\longrightarrow} \ldots \overset{-2}{\longrightarrow} \ldots \overset{-2}{\longrightarrow} \ldots \overset{-2}{\longrightarrow} \ldots$$

You can use the **position-to-term** rule for a sequence to work out any term in the sequence.

2 Write down the first five terms of each sequence in the tables. Some of them have been started for you.

a Position-to-term rule: term = 2 × position number.

You can write the terms out in a table like this.

1st term	2nd term	3rd term	4th term	5th term
2 × 1	2 × 2	2 × 3	2 × 4	2 × ......
2	4	6	......	......

b Position-to-term rule: term = position number + 5.

1st term	2nd term	3rd term	4th term	5th term
1 + 5	2 + 5	3 + 5	...... + 5	...... + 5
6	7	......	......	......

c Position-to-term rule: term = position number – 1.

1st term	2nd term	3rd term	4th term	5th term
1 – 1	...... – 1	...... – 1	...... – 1	...... – 1
0	......	......	......	......

Now try Exercise 2.1 on page 19 of Coursebook 8.

2.2 Finding rules for sequences

You can work out the term-to-term rule and the position-to-term rule of a sequence like this:

For the sequence: 4, 7, 10, 13, 16, ...

Step 1: Work out how you get from one term to the next:

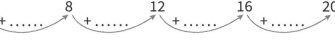

4   +3   7   +3   10   +3   13   +3   16

So the term-to-term rule is 'Add 3'.

Step 2: Make a table like this:

Term number	1st	2nd	3rd	4th	5th
Sequence	4	7	10	13	16
Position × 3	1 × 3 = 3	2 × 3 = 6	3 × 3 = 9	4 × 3 = 12	5 × 3 = 15
Position × 3 + 1	3 + 1 = 4	6 + 1 = 7	9 + 1 = 10	12 + 1 = 13	15 + 1 = 16

> Because the term-to-term rule is 'Add 3', first work out the position numbers × 3.

> The sequence is: 4, 7, 10, 13, 16. Position × 3 gives: 3, 6, 9, 12, 15 so 'Add 1' to position × 3 will give the exact numbers in the sequence.

Step 3: Write down the position-to-term rule: term = position number × 3 + 1

---

1 Complete the workings to find the term-to-term rule and the position-to-term rule of each sequence.

a 4, 8, 12, 16, 20, ...

Step 1: 4   + ...   8   + ...   12   + ...   16   + ...   20   So the term-to-term rule is 'Add ......'

Step 2:

Term number	1st	2nd	3rd	4th	5th
Sequence	4	8	12	16	20
Position × 4	1 × 4 = 4	2 × 4 = ...	3 × 4 = ...	4 × 4 = ...	5 × 4 = ...

Step 3: position-to-term rule   term = position number × ......

b 5, 7, 9, 11, 13 …

Step 1: 5 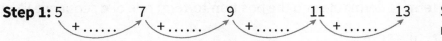 So the term-to-term rule is 'Add ……'

Step 2:

Term number	1st	2nd	3rd	4th	5th
Sequence	5	7	9	11	13
Position × 2	$1 \times 2 = 2$	$2 \times 2 = ……$	$3 \times 2 = …..$	$4 \times 2 = ……$	$5 \times 2 = …..$
Position × 2 + 3	$2 + 3 = 5$	$4 + 3 = ……$	$6 + 3 = ……$	$….. + 3 = ……$	$…… + 3 = ……$

Step 3: position-to-term rule   term = position number × …… + ……

c 6, 11, 16, 21, 26 …

Step 1: 6 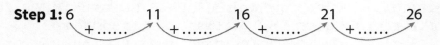 So the term-to-term rule is 'Add ……'

Step 2:

Term number	1st	2nd	3rd	4th	5th
Sequence	6	11	16	21	26
Position × 5	$1 \times 5 = 5$	$2 \times 5 = …..$	$3 \times 5 = …..$	$4 \times 5 = …..$	$5 \times 5 = …..$
Position × 5 + ……	$5 + …..$ $= 6$	$10 + …..$ $= 11$	$….. + ….$ $= 16$	$….. + …..$ $= 21$	$….. + ….$ $= 26$

Step 3: position-to-term rule   term = position number × …… + ……

Now try Exercise 2.2 on page 22 of Coursebook 8.

2.3 Using the *n*th term

The **_n_th** term formula is another way to write the position-to-term rule.

You can work out a sequence using the *n*th term by drawing a table.

When the *n*th term is $2n + 1$, the first five terms are:

Term number (n)	1st	2nd	3rd	4th	5th
2 × n	$2 \times 1 = 2$	$2 \times 2 = 4$	$2 \times 3 = 6$	$2 \times 4 = 8$	$2 \times 5 = 10$
2 × n + 1	$2 + 1 = 3$	$4 + 1 = 5$	$6 + 1 = 7$	$8 + 1 = 9$	$10 + 1 = 11$

So the first five terms of the sequence are 3, 5, 7, 9, 11.

1 Complete the tables to work out the first five terms of each sequence.

a *n*th term is $n + 3$.

Term number (n)	1st	2nd	3rd	4th	5th
n + 3	$1 + 3 = 4$	$2 + 3 = 5$	$3 + 3 = 6$	$4 + 3 = \ldots\ldots$	$5 + 3 = \ldots\ldots$

So the first five terms of the sequence are 4, 5, 6, ... , ...

b *n*th term is $n + 9$

Term number (n)	1st	2nd	3rd	4th	5th
n + 9	$1 + 9 = 10$	$2 + 9 = \ldots\ldots$	$3 + 9 = \ldots\ldots$	$4 + 9 = \ldots\ldots$	$5 + 9 = \ldots\ldots$

So the first five terms of the sequence are 10, ... , ... , ... , ...

c nth term is $n - 2$.

Term number (n)	1st	2nd	3rd	4th	5th
$n - 2$	$1 - 2 = -1$	$2 - 2 = \ldots\ldots$	$3 - 2 = \ldots\ldots$	$4 - 2 = \ldots\ldots$	$5 - 2 = \ldots\ldots$

So the first five terms of the sequence are $-1, \ldots\ldots, \ldots\ldots, \ldots\ldots, \ldots\ldots$

d nth term is $5n$.

Term number (n)	1st	2nd	3rd	4th	5th
$5 \times n$	$5 \times 1 = 5$	$5 \times 2 = \ldots\ldots$	$5 \times 3 = \ldots\ldots$	$5 \times 4 = \ldots\ldots$	$5 \times 5 = \ldots\ldots$

So the first five terms of the sequence are $5, \ldots\ldots, \ldots\ldots, \ldots\ldots, \ldots\ldots$

e nth term is $3n - 1$.

Term number (n)	1st	2nd	3rd	4th	5th
$3 \times n$	$3 \times 1 = 3$	$3 \times 2 = 6$	$3 \times 3 = \ldots\ldots$	$3 \times 4 = \ldots\ldots$	$3 \times 5 = \ldots\ldots$
$3 \times n - 1$	$3 - 1 = 2$	$6 - 1 = 5$	$\ldots\ldots - 1 = \ldots\ldots$	$\ldots\ldots - 1 = \ldots\ldots$	$\ldots\ldots - 1 = \ldots\ldots$

So the first five terms of the sequence are $2, 5, \ldots\ldots, \ldots\ldots, \ldots\ldots$

Now try Exercise 2.3 on page 23 of Coursebook 8.

2.4 Using functions and mappings

Here is a function machine.

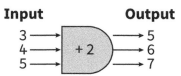

Input   **Output**

3 → +2 → 5
4 → → 6
5 → → 7

> The function is 'Add 2', so 2 is added to each **input** number to give the **output** number.

You can write the input and output numbers in a table like this:

Input	3	4	5
Output	5	6	7

---

1 Find the missing output numbers in each of these function machines.

Write the input and output numbers in the table given.

a **Input**   **Output**

5 → +3 → 8
6 → → ......
7 → → ......

Input	5	6	......
Output	8	......	......

b **Input**   **Output**

5 → −3 → 2
6 → → ......
7 → → ......

Input	5	6	......
Output	2	......	......

A function can be written as an **equation**.

The letter x is used for the input numbers and the letter y for the output numbers, like this:

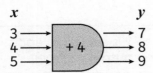

x	3	4	5
y	7	8	9

All the x values + 4 = the y values, which you write as $x + 4 = y$, or $y = x + 4$.

2 Find the missing output numbers in each of these function machines.

Write the input and output numbers in the table, and write the function as an equation.

a Input   Output
2 →
3 → + 6
4 →

Input	2	3	......
Output	......	......	......

Equation:
$y = x + ...$

b Input   Output
10 →
8 → − 5
6 →

Input	10	......	......
Output	......	......	......

Equation:
$y = x − ......$

Now try Exercise 2.4 on page 25 of Coursebook 8.

2.5 **Constructing linear expressions**

You can write an algebraic expression by using a letter to represent an unknown number.

This bag contains x balls. Look at the expressions around the outside of the bag.

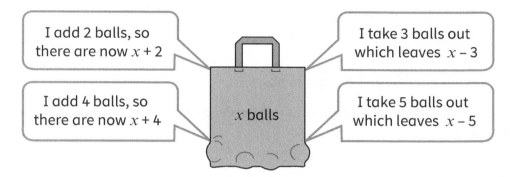

I add 2 balls, so there are now $x + 2$

I add 4 balls, so there are now $x + 4$

x balls

I take 3 balls out which leaves $x - 3$

I take 5 balls out which leaves $x - 5$

1 This bag contains y counters.

y counters

Draw a line joining each statement on the left with the correct expression on the right. One has been done for you.

I add 1 counter to the bag, so there are now $y - 8$

I take 1 counter out of the bag, which leaves $y + 1$

I add 5 counters to the bag, so there are now $y - 5$

I take 5 counters out of the bag, which leaves $y + 8$

I add 8 counters to the bag, so there are now $y + 5$

I take 8 counters out of the bag, which leaves $y - 1$

2 This box contains some books.

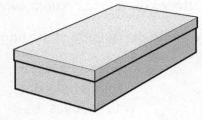

When you double the number, you × by 2.

I double the number of books in the box.

Complete the workings to show how many books are now in the box, when the box started with:

a 3 books: 3 × 2 = ...

b 5 books: 5 × 2 = ...

c 8 books: 8 × ...... = ...

d x books: x × ...... = $2x$

e y books: y × ...... = ...

f b books: b × ...... = ...

3 This tin contains some sweets.

When you halve the number, you ÷ by 2.

I halve the number of sweets in the tin.

Complete the workings to show how many sweets are now in the tin, when the tin started with:

a 4 sweets: 4 ÷ 2 = ...

b 10 sweets: 10 ÷ 2 = ...

c 12 sweets: 12 ÷ ...... = ...

d x sweets: x ÷ ...... = $\dfrac{x}{2}$

e y sweets: y ÷ ...... = $\dfrac{}{2}$

f s sweets: s ÷ ...... = —

Now try Exercise 2.5 on page 26 of Coursebook 8.

2.6 Deriving and using formulae

A **formula** is a mathematical rule that connects two or more quantities. It can be written in letters or words. The plural of formula is **formulae**.

Before you start using formulae you need to be able to substitute numbers into expressions.

1 Draw lines to match each expression with its correct value when $x = 6$.
The first one has been done for you.

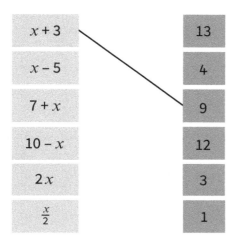

2 Work out the value of these expressions when $x = 4$ and $y = 3$.

a $x + y$ ....

$x + y = 4 + 3 = ?$

b $x - y$ ....

c y^2 ....

$y^2 = y \times y$

When you substitute numbers into an expression or formula, you must use the correct order of operations:

B	I	D	M	A	S
Brackets	**I**ndices (powers)	**D**ivision	**M**ultiplication	**A**ddition	**S**ubtraction

3 Complete the workings to find the value of each expression when $x = 6$.

a $2x + 1$

$2 \times x + 1 = 2 \times 6 + 1$

$\qquad = 12 + 1$

$\qquad = \ldots\ldots$

> Work out the **M**ultiplication before the **A**ddition.

b $3x - 1$

$3 \times x - 1 = 3 \times 6 - 1$

$\qquad = \ldots\ldots - 1$

$\qquad = \ldots\ldots$

> Work out the **M**ultiplication before the **S**ubtraction.

c $2x^2$

$2 \times x^2 = 2 \times 6^2$

$\qquad = 2 \times 36$

$\qquad = \ldots\ldots$

> Work out the **I**ndices before the **M**ultiplication.

d $10 - \dfrac{x}{3}$

$10 - \dfrac{x}{3} = 10 - \dfrac{6}{3}$

$\qquad = 10 - \ldots\ldots$

$\qquad = \ldots\ldots$

> Work out the **D**ivision before the **S**ubtraction.

e $2(x + 4)$

$2 \times (x + 4) = 2 \times (6 + 4)$

$\qquad = 2 \times \ldots\ldots$

$\qquad = \ldots\ldots$

> Work out the **B**racket before the **M**ultiplication.

Now try Exercise 2.6 on page 27 of Coursebook 8.

3.1 Multiplying and dividing by 0.1 and 0.01

The numbers 10, 100, 1000, 10 000, ... can all be written as **powers of 10**.

The power of 10 is the number of 10s that you multiply together to get the number.

---

1 Draw a line from each rectangular card to its matching oval card. One has been done for you.

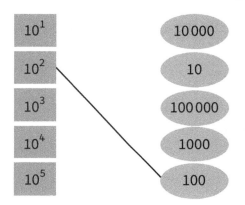

> The power tells you the number of zeros after the 1, so
>
> $10^2 = 100$ (two zeros after the 1).

Look at the rule in this cloud.

$\times \mathbf{0.1}$ is the same as $\div \mathbf{10}$ → e.g. $60 \times \mathbf{0.1} = 60 \div \mathbf{10} = 6$

2 Complete the workings.

a $20 \times 0.1 = 20 \div 10 = \ldots\ldots$

b $70 \times 0.1 = 70 \div \ldots\ldots = \ldots\ldots$

c $80 \times 0.1 = 80 \div \ldots\ldots = \ldots\ldots$

d $75 \times 0.1 = 75 \div \ldots\ldots = \ldots\ldots$

$\times \mathbf{0.01}$ is the same as $\div \mathbf{100}$ → e.g. $600 \times \mathbf{0.01} = 600 \div \mathbf{100} = 6$

3 Complete the workings.

a $300 \times 0.01 = 300 \div 100 = \ldots\ldots$

b $500 \times 0.01 = 500 \div \ldots\ldots = \ldots\ldots$

c $600 \times 0.01 = 600 \div \ldots\ldots = \ldots\ldots$

d $650 \times 0.01 = 650 \div \ldots\ldots = \ldots\ldots$

÷ **0.1** is the same as × **10** → e.g. $6 ÷ \mathbf{0.1} = 6 × \mathbf{10} = 60$

4 Complete the workings.

a $4 ÷ 0.1 = 4 × 10 = \ldots\ldots$

b $7 ÷ 0.1 = 7 × \ldots\ldots = \ldots\ldots$

c $20 ÷ 0.1 = 20 × \ldots\ldots = \ldots\ldots$

d $25 ÷ 0.1 = 25 × \ldots\ldots = \ldots\ldots$

÷ **0.01** is the same as × **100** → e.g. $6 ÷ \mathbf{0.01} = 6 × \mathbf{100} = 600$

5 Complete the workings.

a $2 ÷ 0.01 = 2 × 100 = \ldots\ldots$

b $5 ÷ 0.01 = 5 × \ldots\ldots = \ldots\ldots$

c $30 ÷ 0.01 = 30 × \ldots\ldots = \ldots\ldots$

d $12 ÷ 0.01 = 12 × \ldots\ldots = \ldots\ldots$

Now try Exercise 3.1 on page 33 of Coursebook 8.

3.2 Ordering decimals

When you order decimal numbers, first compare the whole number part:

(9)45   (2)45   (5)76   (3)12   (8)05

When they are all different you can order them straight away:

2.45   3.12   5.76   8.05   9.45

> Write just the whole numbers in order first: 2, 3, 5, 8, 9.

---

1 Write these decimal numbers in order of size, starting with the smallest.

| 17.3 | 4.2 | 3.6 | 15.5 | 12.9 |

> Follow the method in the example above.

....

2 **a** Write these measurements in the correct spaces under the ruler.

9.4 cm   9.8 cm   9.2 cm   9.7 cm   9.5 cm

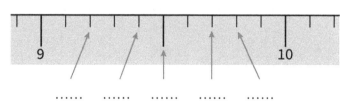

....

b Write these numbers in order of size, starting with the smallest.

9.4   9.8   9.2   9.7   9.5

....

....

c Write these numbers in order of size, starting with the smallest.

12.7   12.9   12.6   12.1   12.4

....

....

Use the following method to order decimal numbers with different numbers of decimal places.

Example: 9.5   9.12   9.35   9.1

> They all have the same whole number, 9.

First, rewrite all the numbers so they have two decimal places:

> Add zeros if you need to.

9.50   9.12   9.35   9.10

Order the numbers after the decimal point: 10   12   35   50

Write the numbers in the correct order: 9.10   9.12   9.35   9.50

3 Write these numbers in order of size, starting with the smallest.

> Follow the method in the example above.

a 4.7   4.23   4.09   4.4

....

....

....

b 8.16   8.1   8.09   8.9

....

....

....

Now try Exercise 3.2 on page 34 of Coursebook 8.

3.3 Adding and subtracting decimals

This is an example of how to add two decimal numbers.

You must keep the decimal points in line.

Start with the tenths: 8 + 4 = 12.

Then the units: 6 + 7 + 1 = 14.

Finally the tens: 5 + 1 = 6.

Tens	Units	Point	Tenths
5	6	.	8
+	7	.	4
6	4	.	2
1	1		

---

1 Work out the answers to these decimal additions. Some have been started for you.

> Remember to start from the right – add the tenths first, then the units, etc.

a
```
    8 . 3
+　1 . 6
─────────
      . 9
```

b
```
    5 . 4
+　6 . 8
─────────
      . 2
     1
```

c
```
    9 . 7
+　0 . 9
─────────
      .
```

d
```
  2 8 . 6
+ 1 3 . 1
─────────
       .
```

e
```
  4 4 . 7
+     9 . 6
─────────
       .
```

f
```
  8 6 . 9
+ 5 2 . 3
─────────
       .
```

2 Work out the answers to these decimal additions. Some have been started for you.

a 2.45 + 3.32
```
  2 . 4 5
+ 3 . 3 2
─────────
    .
```

b 5.63 + 6.18
```
  5 . 6 3
+   .
─────────
    .
```

c 9.6 + 7.48
```
  9 . 6 0
+   .
─────────
    .
```

d 12.72 + 6.4
```
        .
+ 0 6 . 4 0
─────────
        .
```

> Line up the decimal points in each question so they are underneath each other. Fill in empty spaces with zeros.

3 Work out the answers to these decimal subtractions.
Some have been started for you.

> Remember to start from the right.

a
```
    8 . 7
  - 5 . 6
  ───────
      . 1
```

b
```
  ₆⁵ . ¹4
  - 3 . 6
  ───────
      . 8
```

c
```
    4 . 5
  - 0 . 8
  ───────
      .
```

d
```
   3 2 . 7
 - 1 0 . 4
 ─────────
       .
```

e
```
   4 ₅⁴ . ¹2
  -    3 . 5
  ──────────
         .
```

f
```
   3 ₅⁴ . ¹4
  - 2 9 . 5
  ──────────
         .
```

4 Work out the answers to these decimal subtractions.
Some have been started for you.

a 4.76 – 2.34
```
    4 . 7 6
  - 2 . 3 4
  ─────────
        .
```

b 3.97 – 2.8
```
        .
  - 2 . 8 0
  ─────────
        .
```

c 8.5 – 4.12
```
    8 . 5 0
  -     .
  ─────────
        .
```

d 25.63 – 4.9
```
          .
  - 0 4 . 9 0
  ───────────
          .
```

Now try Exercise 3.4 on page 37 of Coursebook 8.

3.4 Dividing decimals

Here is one method of dividing 96 by 4.

Step 1: $9 \div 4 = 2$ → 2 4 ← **Step 2:** $16 \div 4 = 4$
remainder 1 →
$$4 \overline{) 9 \, {}^16}$$

So $96 \div 4 = 24$

You can use the same method to divide 9.6 by 4, but you must include the decimal point.

$$4 \overline{) \begin{array}{c} 2 \cdot 4 \\ 9 \cdot {}^16 \end{array}}$$

So $9.6 \div 4 = 2.4$

---

1 Complete these divisions. Some of them have been started for you.

a
  i $3 \overline{) \begin{array}{c} 3 \\ 9 \ 6 \end{array}}$ **ii** $3 \overline{) \begin{array}{c} \ \ \cdot \\ 9 \ . \ 6 \end{array}}$

b
  i $2 \overline{) 4 \ 8}$ **ii** $2 \overline{) \begin{array}{c} \ \ \cdot \\ 4 \ . \ 8 \end{array}}$

c
  i $4 \overline{) \begin{array}{c} 1 \\ 5 \ {}^12 \end{array}}$ **ii** $4 \overline{) \begin{array}{c} 1 \ . \\ 5 \ . \ {}^12 \end{array}}$

d
  i $6 \overline{) 8 \ 4}$ **ii** $6 \overline{) \begin{array}{c} \ \ \cdot \\ 8 \ . \ 4 \end{array}}$

2 Complete these divisions. Some of them have been started for you.

a
  i $2 \overline{) \begin{array}{c} 2 \ 3 \\ 4 \ 6 \ 2 \end{array}}$ **ii** $2 \overline{) \begin{array}{c} \ \ \ \cdot \\ 4 \ 6 \ . \ 2 \end{array}}$ **iii** $2 \overline{) \begin{array}{c} \ \cdot \\ 4 \ . \ 6 \ 2 \end{array}}$ **iv** $2 \overline{) \begin{array}{c} 0 \ . \\ 0 \ . \ 4 \ 6 \ 2 \end{array}}$

b
  i $3 \overline{) \begin{array}{c} 2 \ 1 \\ 6 \ 5 \ {}^24 \end{array}}$ **ii** $3 \overline{) \begin{array}{c} \ \ \ \cdot \\ 6 \ 5 \ . \ 4 \end{array}}$ **iii** $3 \overline{) \begin{array}{c} \ \cdot \\ 6 \ . \ 5 \ 4 \end{array}}$ **iv** $3 \overline{) \begin{array}{c} 0 \ . \\ 0 \ . \ 6 \ 5 \ 4 \end{array}}$

c
  i $5 \overline{) 7 \ 2 \ 5}$ **ii** $5 \overline{) \begin{array}{c} \ \ \ \cdot \\ 7 \ 2 \ . \ 5 \end{array}}$ **iii** $5 \overline{) \begin{array}{c} \ \cdot \\ 7 \ . \ 2 \ 5 \end{array}}$ **iv** $5 \overline{) \begin{array}{c} \ \cdot \\ 0 \ . \ 7 \ 2 \ 5 \end{array}}$

3 Round each of these numbers correct to one decimal place.

a 4.61 . . . .

> 4.61 rounds down to 4.6,
> but 4.69 rounds up to 4.?

b 4.69 . . . .

c 8.23 . . . .

d 8.25 . . . .

Not all divisions work out exactly. If you are asked to give your answer to one decimal place, work out the answer to two decimal places and then round your answer to one decimal place.

$$
\begin{array}{r}
1\ \ 9\ .\ \ 3\ \ 3 \\
3\overline{)5\ \ {}^{2}8\ .\ {}^{1}0\ {}^{1}0}
\end{array}
$$

Example: 58 ÷ 3   58 ÷ 3 = 19.3 to one decimal place

4 Work out this division. Give your answer correct to one decimal place.

$$
7\overline{)8\ \ 9\ .\ 0\ \ 0}
$$

89 ÷ 7   89 ÷ 7 = ... to one decimal place

Now try Exercise 3.5 on page 38 of Coursebook 8.

3.5 Multiplying by decimals

You already know that multiplying a number by 0.1 is the same as dividing the number by 10.

> × **0.1** is the same as ÷ **10**

1 Look at these rules.

> × **0.2** is the same as ÷ **10** and × **2**

> × **0.3** is the same as ÷ **10** and × **3**

Follow the pattern to complete these rules.

a × **0.4** is the same as ÷ **10** and × ......

b × **0.5** is the same as ÷ **10** and × ......

One way to multiply a number by 0.2 is to divide the number by 10, then multiply by 2.

> × **0.2** is the same as ÷ **10** and × **2**

e.g. 60 × **0.2** =
60 ÷ **10** = 6 × **2** = 12

2 Complete the workings.

a 30 × 0.2   30 ÷ 10 = 3 × 2 = ...

b 40 × 0.2   40 ÷ ...... = ... × 2 = ...

c 12 × 0.2   12 ÷ 10 = 1.2 × ...... = ...

One way to multiply a number by 0.3 is to divide the number by 10, then multiply by 3.

> × **0.3** is the same as ÷ **10** and × **3**

e.g. 60 × **0.3** =
60 ÷ **10** = 6 × **3** = 18

3 Complete the workings.

a 30×0.3 $30 \div 10 = 3 \times 3 = \ldots\ldots$

b 50×0.3 $50 \div \ldots\ldots = \ldots\ldots \times 3 = \ldots\ldots$

c 15×0.3 $15 \div 10 = 1.5 \times \ldots\ldots = \ldots\ldots$

One way to multiply a number by 0.02 is to divide the number by 100, then multiply by 2.

$\times$ **0.02** is the same as $\div$ **100** and $\times$ **2**

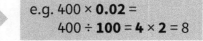

e.g. $400 \times$ **0.02** $=$
$400 \div$ **100** $= $ **4** $\times$ **2** $= 8$

4 Complete the workings.

a 500×0.02 $500 \div 100 = 5 \times 2 = \ldots\ldots$

b 600×0.02 $600 \div \ldots\ldots = \ldots\ldots \times 2 = \ldots\ldots$

c 250×0.02 $250 \div 100 = 2.5 \times \ldots\ldots = \ldots\ldots$

One way to multiply a number by 0.03 is to divide the number by 100, then multiply by 3.

$\times$ **0.03** is the same as $\div$ **100** and $\times$ **3**

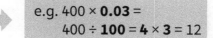

e.g. $400 \times$ **0.03** $=$
$400 \div$ **100** $= $ **4** $\times$ **3** $= 12$

5 Complete the workings.

a 200×0.03 $200 \div 100 = 2 \times 3 = \ldots..$

b 700×0.03 $700 \div \ldots.. = \ldots.. \times 3 = \ldots..$

c 120×0.03 $120 \div 100 = 1.2 \times \ldots.. = \ldots..$

Now try Exercise 3.6 on page 39 of Coursebook 8.

3.6 Dividing by decimals

You already know that dividing a number by 0.1 is the same as multiplying the number by 10.

> ÷ **0.1** is the same as × **10**

---

1 Look at these rules.

> ÷ **0.2** is the same as × **10** and ÷ **2**

> ÷ **0.3** is the same as × **10** and ÷ **3**

Follow the pattern to complete these rules.

a ÷ 0.4 is the same as × 10 and ÷ . . . . . .   **b** ÷ 0.5 is the same as × 10 and ÷ . . . . . .

One way to divide a number by 0.2 is to multiply the number by 10, then divide by 2.

> ÷ **0.2** is the same as × **10** and ÷ **2** ⟶ e.g. 6 ÷ **0.2** = 6 × **10** = 60 ÷ **2** = 30

2 Complete the workings.

a 3 ÷ 0.2   3 × 10 = 30 ÷ 2 = ...

b 4 ÷ 0.2   4 × . . . . . . = ... ÷ 2 = ...

c 1.4 ÷ 0.2   1.4 × 10 = 14 ÷ . . . . . . = ...

One way to divide a number by 0.3 is to multiply the number by 10, then divide by 3.

> ÷ **0.3** is the same as × **10** and ÷ **3** ⟶ e.g. 6 ÷ **0.3** = 6 × **10** = 60 ÷ **3** = 20

3 Complete the workings.

a $6 \div 0.3$ $6 \times 10 = 60 \div 3 = \ldots\ldots$

b $9 \div 0.3$ $9 \times \ldots\ldots = \ldots\ldots \div 3 = \ldots\ldots$

c $1.2 \div 0.3$ $1.2 \times 10 = 12 \div \ldots\ldots = \ldots\ldots$

One way to divide a number by 0.02 is to multiply the number by 100, then divide by 2.

$\div$ **0.02** is the same as $\times$ **100** and $\div$ **2**

e.g. $4 \div$ **0.02** =
$4 \times$ **100** $= 400 \div 2 = 200$

4 Complete the workings.

a $4 \div 0.02$ $4 \times 100 = 400 \div 2 = \ldots\ldots$

b $5 \div 0.02$ $5 \times \ldots\ldots = \ldots\ldots \div 2 = \ldots\ldots$

c $1.8 \div 0.02$ $1.8 \times 100 = 180 \div \ldots\ldots = \ldots\ldots$

One way to divide a number by 0.03 is to multiply the number by 100, then divide by 3.

$\div$ **0.03** is the same as $\times$ **100** and $\div$ **3**

e.g. $6 \div$ **0.03** =
$6 \times$ **100** $= 600 \div 3 = 200$

5 Complete the workings.

a $9 \div 0.03$ $9 \times 100 = 900 \div 3 = \ldots\ldots$

b $15 \div 0.03$ $15 \times \ldots\ldots = \ldots\ldots \div 3 = \ldots\ldots$

c $2.1 \div 0.03$ $2.1 \times 100 = 210 \div \ldots\ldots = \ldots\ldots$

Now try Exercise 3.7 on page 40 of Coursebook 8.

4 Length, mass and capacity

4.1 Kilometres and miles

Distances can be measured in **kilometres** or **miles**.

1 mile is further than 1 kilometre.

1 mile

1 kilometre

---

1 Circle the longest distance. The first one has been done for you.

a (1 mile) or 1 kilometre   **b** 3 miles or 3 kilometres

c 5 miles or 5 kilometres   **d** 10 miles or 10 kilometres

5 miles is about the same distance as 8 kilometres.

5 miles
8 kilometres

2 Follow the pattern to complete the table.

Number of miles	5	10	15	20	25	30	35	40
Number of kilometres	8	16	24	32				

3 This flow chart converts kilometres to miles.

Number of km	÷ 8	× 5	Number of miles

Use the flow chart to convert the following kilometres to miles.

a 16 km $\quad$ $16 \div 8 = 2$ $\quad\quad\quad$ $2 \times 5 = \ldots\ldots$ miles

b 48 km $\quad$ $48 \div 8 = \ldots\ldots$ $\quad\quad$ $\ldots\ldots \times 5 = \ldots\ldots$ miles

c 64 km $\quad$ $64 \div \ldots\ldots = \ldots\ldots$ $\quad$ $\ldots\ldots \times 5 = \ldots\ldots$ miles

d 80 km $\quad$ $80 \div \ldots\ldots = \ldots\ldots$ $\quad$ $\ldots\ldots \times \ldots\ldots = \ldots\ldots$ miles

> Check your answers to parts a), b) and c) in the table in Question 2.

4 This flow chart converts miles to kilometres.

Number of miles	÷ 5	× 8	Number of km

Use the flow chart to convert the following miles to kilometres.

a 15 miles $\quad$ $15 \div 5 = 3$ $\quad\quad\quad$ $3 \times 8 = \ldots\ldots$ km

b 35 miles $\quad$ $35 \div 5 = \ldots\ldots$ $\quad\quad$ $\ldots \times 8 = \ldots\ldots$ km

c 60 miles $\quad$ $60 \div \ldots\ldots = \ldots\ldots$ $\quad$ $\ldots\ldots \times 8 = \ldots\ldots$ km

d 100 miles $\quad$ $100 \div \ldots\ldots = \ldots\ldots$ $\quad$ $\ldots\ldots \times \ldots\ldots = \ldots\ldots$ km

> Check your answers to parts a) and b) in the table in Question 2.

Now try Exercise 4.2 on page 47 of Coursebook 8.

5 Angles

5.1 Parallel lines

Look at this diagram. There are three parallel lines.

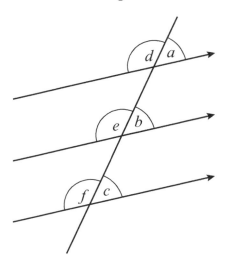

Angles a, b and c are called **corresponding angles**.

Angles d, e and f are corresponding angles.

> Corresponding angles are the same size.

---

1 Look at this diagram, then complete the pairs.

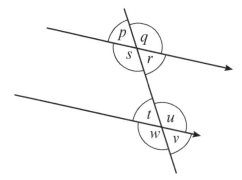

a p and ...... are corresponding angles.

b u and ...... are corresponding angles.

c r and ...... are corresponding angles.

d w and ...... are corresponding angles.

Look at this diagram. It has two parallel lines.

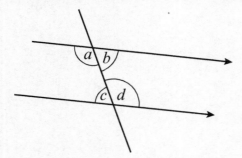

Angles *b* and *c* are called **alternate angles**.

Angles *a* and *d* are alternate angles.

> Alternate angles are the same size.

2 This diagram has three parallel lines.

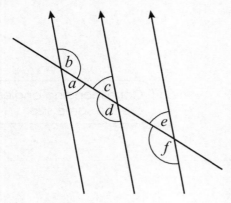

Complete these pairs.

a *c* and ...... are alternate angles.

b *d* and ...... are alternate angles.

c *e* and ...... are alternate angles.

d *f* and ...... are alternate angles.

3 Look at this diagram, then write whether each pair of angles is corresponding or alternate.

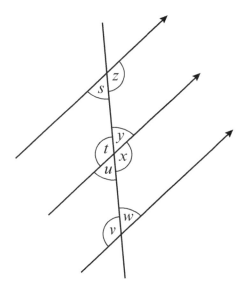

a *s* and *y* are .... angles.   **b** *t* and *v* are .... angles.

c *x* and *z* are .... angles.   **d** *w* and *u* are .... angles.

4 This diagram has two parallel lines.

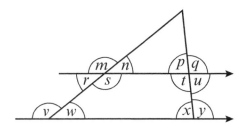

Complete these pairs.

a *r* and ...... are alternate angles.   **b** *p* and ...... are corresponding angles.

c *x* and ...... are alternate angles.   **d** *y* and ...... are corresponding angles.

e *v* and ...... are corresponding angles.   **f** *v* and ...... are alternate angles.

Now try Exercise 5.1 on page 52 of Coursebook 8.

5.2 Explaining angle properties

The angles on a straight line add up to 180°.

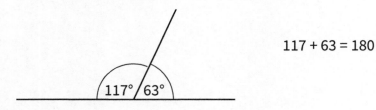

$$117 + 63 = 180$$

The angles of a triangle add up to 180°.

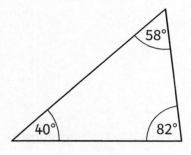

$$58 + 40 + 82 = 180$$

The angles round a point add up to 360°.

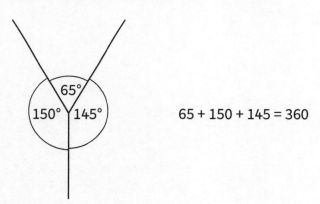

$$65 + 150 + 145 = 360$$

You can use these facts to explain how to find angles.
For example, what is the third angle in this triangle?

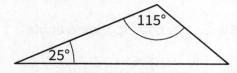

Answer: 40°

$$25 + 115 = 140; 180 - 140 = 40$$

Reason: the three angles of a triangle add up to 180°.

1 Find the missing angle and complete the explanation.

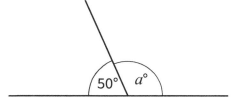

$a = \ldots\ldots\ldots\ldots$

Reason: ....

2 Find the missing angle and complete the explanation.

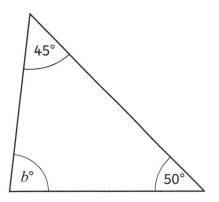

$b = \ldots\ldots\ldots\ldots$

Reason: ....

3 Find the missing angle and complete the explanation.

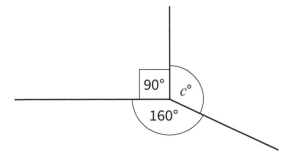

$c = \ldots\ldots\ldots\ldots$

Reason: ....

4 Find the missing angle and complete the explanation.

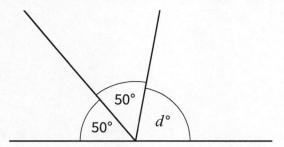

$d =$ . . . .

Reason: . . . .

5 Find the missing angle and complete the explanation.

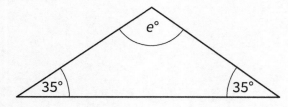

$e =$ . . . .

Reason: . . . .

6 Find the missing angle and complete the explanation.

All three angles are the same size.

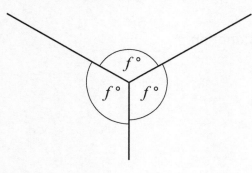

$f =$ . . . .

Reason: . . . .

7 Find the missing angles and complete the explanations.

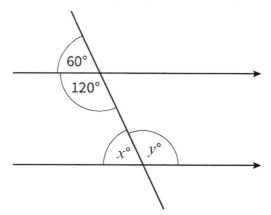

Think about whether they are corresponding angles or alternate angles.

a $x =$ .... Reason: .... angles are equal.

b $y =$ .... Reason: .... angles are equal.

8 Find the missing angles and complete the explanations.

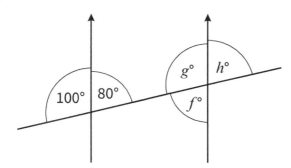

a $f =$ .... Reason: .... angles are equal.

b $g =$ .... Reason: .... angles are equal.

c $h =$ .... Reason: .... angles are equal.

Now try Exercise 5.2 on page 55 of Coursebook 8.

6 Planning and collecting data

6.1 Using frequency tables

This frequency table shows the ages of 15 adults.

This box shows that a represents age.

This box shows that this row is for the adults who are more than 20 years old, but less than or equal to 30 years old.

Age, a (years)	Tally	Frequency
$20 < a \leqslant 30$	卌 I	6
$30 < a \leqslant 40$	IIII	4
$40 < a \leqslant 50$	卌	5

---

1 Look at the frequency table above. Fill in the missing numbers in these sentences.

a The $30 < a \leqslant 40$ group is for the adults who are more than ...... years old, but less than or equal to ...... years old.

b The $40 < a \leqslant 50$ group is for the adults who are more than ...... years old, but less than or equal to ...... years old.

2 This frequency table is for recording the height, h, of some plants.

Height, h (cm)	Tally	Frequency
$0 < h \leqslant 5$		
$5 < h \leqslant 10$	I	
$10 < h \leqslant 15$		
$15 < h \leqslant 20$		

a Fill in the missing numbers in these sentences.

i The $0 < h \leqslant 5$ group is for the plants which are more than ...... cm, but less than or equal to ...... cm.

ii The $5 < h \leqslant 10$ group is for the plants which are more than ...... cm, but less than or equal to ...... cm.

b Circle the group you would put each of these plants in. The first one has been done for you.

   i 8 cm $5 < h \leqslant 10$ or $10 < h \leqslant 15$

   ii 13 cm $5 < h \leqslant 10$ or $10 < h \leqslant 15$

   iii 5 cm $0 < h \leqslant 5$ or $5 < h \leqslant 10$

   iv 15 cm $10 < h \leqslant 15$ or $15 < h \leqslant 20$

c Put a tally for each of these heights in the frequency table at the start of this question. As you record each number, cross it off the list below. The first one has been done for you.

8 cm	13 cm	5 cm	15 cm	4 cm	3 cm	10 cm
12 cm	11 cm	2 cm	16 cm	20 cm	6 cm	19 cm

d When you have entered all the tallies in the table, complete the frequency column.

Now try Exercise 6.3 on page 67 of Coursebook 8.

7 Fractions

7.1 Finding equivalent fractions, decimals and percentages

You need to remember these common equivalent fractions, decimals and percentages:

$25\% = 0.25 = \dfrac{1}{4}$ $50\% = 0.5 = \dfrac{1}{2}$ $75\% = 0.75 = \dfrac{3}{4}$

$20\% = 0.2 = \dfrac{1}{5}$ $40\% = 0.4 = \dfrac{2}{5}$ $60\% = 0.6 = \dfrac{3}{5}$ $80\% = 0.8 = \dfrac{4}{5}$

$10\% = 0.1 = \dfrac{1}{10}$ $30\% = 0.3 = \dfrac{3}{10}$ $70\% = 0.7 = \dfrac{7}{10}$ $90\% = 0.9 = \dfrac{9}{10}$

---

1 Look at the equivalent fractions, decimals and percentages above.

Now cover them up with your hand or a piece of paper.

Use a pencil to join each fraction below to its equivalent percentage and decimal. The first one has been done for you.

20%	0.75	$\dfrac{3}{10}$
10%	0.3	$\dfrac{1}{5}$
75%	0.2	$\dfrac{7}{10}$
90%	0.7	$\dfrac{3}{4}$
30%	0.1	$\dfrac{4}{5}$
25%	0.8	$\dfrac{9}{10}$
80%	0.5	$\dfrac{2}{5}$
40%	0.9	$\dfrac{3}{5}$
70%	0.6	$\dfrac{1}{4}$
50%	0.4	$\dfrac{1}{10}$
60%	0.25	$\dfrac{1}{2}$

2 Fill in the spaces in the following conversions.

$$0.19 = 19\% = \frac{19}{100}$$

a $0.13 = \ldots\ldots\% = \dfrac{13}{100}$

b $0.27 = \ldots\ldots\% = \dfrac{}{100}$

c $\ldots\ldots = 51\% = \dfrac{}{100}$

d $\ldots\ldots = 31\% = \dfrac{}{100}$

e $\ldots\ldots = \ldots\ldots\% = \dfrac{11}{100}$

f $\ldots\ldots = \ldots\ldots\% = \dfrac{63}{100}$

g $0.03 = \ldots\ldots\% = \dfrac{}{100}$

h $\ldots\ldots = \ldots\ldots\% = \dfrac{7}{100}$

3 Complete the workings to write these percentages as fractions.

a $14\% = \dfrac{14}{100} = \dfrac{14 \div 2}{100 \div 2} = \dfrac{}{50}$

b $26\% = \dfrac{26}{100} = \dfrac{26 \div 2}{100 \div 2} = \dfrac{}{}$

c $32\% = \dfrac{32}{100} = \dfrac{32 \div 4}{100 \div 4} = \dfrac{}{}$

d $56\% = \dfrac{56}{100} = \dfrac{56 \div 4}{100 \div 4} = \dfrac{}{}$

4 Complete the workings to write these decimals as fractions.

a $0.46 = \dfrac{46}{100} = \dfrac{46 \div 2}{100 \div 2} = \dfrac{}{50}$

b $22\% = \dfrac{22}{100} = \dfrac{22 \div 2}{100 \div 2} = \dfrac{}{}$

c $0.08 = \dfrac{8}{100} = \dfrac{8 \div 4}{100 \div 4} = \dfrac{}{}$

d $0.84 = \dfrac{84}{100} = \dfrac{84 \div 4}{100 \div 4} = \dfrac{}{}$

Now try Exercise 7.1 on page 72 of Coursebook 8.

7.2 Ordering fractions

You can write fractions **in order of size** by comparing them using diagrams.

You can also compare them using equivalent fractions with the same denominator.

1 In each part of this question:

   i Shade in the fraction stated for each rectangle.

   ii Write which fraction is smaller.

> Always shade the rectangles from the left, so that it is easy to compare the shaded sections.

a

$\dfrac{2}{3}$

$\dfrac{3}{5}$

.... is the smaller fraction

b

$\dfrac{4}{7}$

$\dfrac{3}{8}$

.... is the smaller fraction

c

$\dfrac{7}{10}$

$\dfrac{3}{4}$

.... is the smaller fraction

d

$\dfrac{5}{6}$

$\dfrac{7}{9}$

.... is the smaller fraction

2 In each part of this question:

   i Complete the working to find the equivalent fraction.

   ii Shade in the fraction stated for each rectangle.

   iii Write which fraction is smaller.

a

$\dfrac{3}{8}$

$\dfrac{1}{4}$ $\dfrac{1}{4} = \dfrac{1 \times 2}{4 \times 2} = \dfrac{}{8}$

.... is the smaller fraction

> Shade three out of the eight sections of the first rectangle, then two out of the eight sections of the second rectangle and then compare.

b 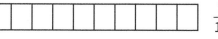 $\dfrac{9}{10}$

$\dfrac{4}{5}$ $\dfrac{4}{5} = \dfrac{4 \times 2}{5 \times 2} = -$

.... is the smaller fraction

c $\dfrac{4}{5}$ $\dfrac{4}{5} = \dfrac{4 \times 3}{5 \times 3} = -$

$\dfrac{11}{15}$

.... is the smaller fraction

3 Write the fractions in each part as equivalent fractions with a common denominator.

Write the fractions in order, starting with the smallest. Some have been started for you.

a $\dfrac{1}{2}$ $\dfrac{1}{3}$ $\dfrac{5}{6}$

$\dfrac{1}{2} = \dfrac{1 \times 3}{2 \times 3} = \dfrac{3}{6}$ $\dfrac{1}{3} = \dfrac{1 \times 2}{3 \times 2} = \dfrac{}{6}$ $\dfrac{5}{6} = \dfrac{5}{6}$

> The common denominator for 2, 3 and 6 is 6.

In order of size: $\dfrac{2}{6}, \dfrac{3}{6}, \dfrac{5}{6}$

Using the original fractions: $\dfrac{1}{3}, -, -$

b $\dfrac{2}{3}$ $\dfrac{4}{9}$ $\dfrac{11}{18}$

$\dfrac{2}{3} = \dfrac{2 \times 6}{3 \times 6} = \dfrac{}{18}$ $\dfrac{4}{9} = \dfrac{4 \times 2}{9 \times 2} = \dfrac{}{18}$ $\dfrac{11}{18} = \dfrac{}{}$

> The common denominator for 3, 9 and 18 is 18.

In order of size: $\dfrac{}{18}, \dfrac{}{18}, \dfrac{}{18}$

Using the original fractions: $-, -, -$

Now try Exercise 7.3 on page 74 of Coursebook 8.

7.3 Adding and subtracting fractions

You can only add or subtract fractions when the denominators are the same.

1. Draw a line linking each calculation to its correct answer.

$\frac{1}{5} + \frac{1}{5}$	$\frac{5}{7}$
$\frac{8}{11} - \frac{1}{11}$	$\frac{7}{8}$
$\frac{2}{7} + \frac{3}{7}$	$\frac{7}{11}$
$\frac{5}{9} - \frac{4}{9}$	$\frac{4}{7}$
$\frac{3}{8} + \frac{4}{8}$	$\frac{1}{3}$
$\frac{2}{3} - \frac{1}{3}$	$\frac{2}{5}$
$\frac{6}{7} - \frac{2}{7}$	$\frac{1}{9}$

2. Work out these additions and subtractions by changing the fractions to equivalent fractions.

   a. $\frac{1}{2} + \frac{1}{4} = \frac{2}{4} + \frac{1}{4} = \frac{\ }{4}$

   Change $\frac{1}{2}$ to $\frac{2}{4}$ like this $\frac{1 \times 2}{2 \times 2} = \frac{2}{4}$

   b. $\frac{9}{10} - \frac{3}{5} = \frac{9}{10} - \frac{\ }{10} = \frac{\ }{10}$

   c. $\frac{1}{6} + \frac{2}{3} = \frac{1}{6} + \frac{\ }{6} = \frac{\ }{6}$

   d. $\frac{3}{4} - \frac{2}{3} = \frac{\ }{12} - \frac{\ }{12} = \frac{\ }{12}$

   Change $\frac{3}{4}$ and $\frac{2}{3}$ like this $\frac{3 \times 3}{4 \times 3} = \frac{?}{12}$, $\frac{2 \times 4}{3 \times 4} = \frac{?}{12}$

   e. $\frac{1}{2} + \frac{2}{5} = \frac{\ }{10} + \frac{\ }{10} = \frac{\ }{10}$

   f. $\frac{1}{5} + \frac{2}{3} = \frac{\ }{15} + \frac{\ }{15} = \frac{\ }{15}$

3 Change these **improper fractions** into mixed numbers. Use the diagrams to help you.

a $\dfrac{3}{2} = 1\dfrac{}{2}$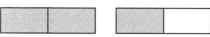

b $\dfrac{5}{3} = 1\dfrac{}{3}$

c $\dfrac{7}{4} = 1\dfrac{}{4}$

d $\dfrac{7}{5} = 1\dfrac{}{5}$

4 Work out these additions. Give each answer as a mixed number. The first one has been done for you.

> You can draw a diagram to help you.

a $\dfrac{2}{3} + \dfrac{2}{3} = \dfrac{4}{3}, \dfrac{4}{3} = 1\dfrac{1}{3}$

b $\dfrac{2}{5} + \dfrac{4}{5} = \dfrac{}{5}, \dfrac{}{5} = 1\dfrac{}{5}$

c $\dfrac{4}{7} + \dfrac{5}{7} = \dfrac{}{7}, \dfrac{}{7} = 1\dfrac{}{7}$

d $\dfrac{8}{9} + \dfrac{5}{9} = \dfrac{}{9}, \dfrac{}{9} = 1\dfrac{}{9}$

5 Work out these additions by changing the fractions to equivalent fractions.

Write each answer as a mixed number.

a $\dfrac{7}{8} + \dfrac{1}{4} = \dfrac{7}{8} + \dfrac{}{8} = \dfrac{}{8} = 1\dfrac{}{8}$

b $\dfrac{5}{6} + \dfrac{1}{3} = \dfrac{5}{6} + \dfrac{}{6} = \dfrac{}{6} = 1\dfrac{}{6}$

c $\dfrac{3}{4} + \dfrac{4}{5} = \dfrac{}{20} + \dfrac{}{20} = \dfrac{}{20} = 1\dfrac{}{20}$

Now try Exercise 7.4 on page 76 of Coursebook 8.

7.4 Finding fractions of a quantity

You work out a unit fraction of an amount by dividing the amount by the denominator.

$\frac{1}{2}$ of 18 kg = 18 ÷ 2 = 9 kg

$\frac{1}{3}$ of 18 kg = 18 ÷ 3 = 6 kg

A unit fraction has a numerator of 1. $\frac{1}{2}, \frac{1}{3}$ and $\frac{1}{4}$ are all unit fractions.

1 Complete the workings to find the unit fraction of each amount.

a $\frac{1}{2}$ of 12 kg = 12 ÷ 2 = ... kg

b $\frac{1}{3}$ of 9 km = 9 ÷ ...... = ... km

c $\frac{1}{4}$ of 20 cm = ... ÷ ..... = ... cm

d $\frac{1}{5}$ of 20 mm = ... ÷ ...... = ... mm

e $\frac{1}{2}$ of 8 m = ... ÷ ...... = ... m

f $\frac{1}{6}$ of 30 m = ... ÷ ...... = ... m

Follow this rule to work out a fraction of an amount:

Amount → ÷ by denominator → × by numerator → = answer

Remember: $\frac{\text{numerator}}{\text{denominator}}$

2 Complete the workings to find the fraction of each amount.

a $\frac{2}{3}$ of 9 kg $\frac{1}{3}$ of 9 kg = 9 ÷ 3 = 3 kg   so $\frac{2}{3}$ of 9 kg = 3 × 2 = ... kg

b $\frac{3}{4}$ of 20 km $\frac{1}{4}$ of 20 km = 20 ÷ 4 = ... km   so $\frac{3}{4}$ of 20 km = ... × 3 = ... km

c $\frac{2}{5}$ of 35 m $\frac{1}{5}$ of 35 m = ... ÷ ...... = ... m   so $\frac{2}{5}$ of 35 m = ... × ...... = ... m

d $\frac{4}{7}$ of 42 t $\frac{1}{7}$ of 42 t = ... ÷ ...... = ... t   so $\frac{4}{7}$ of 42 t = ... × ...... = ... t

3 When the amount cannot be divided exactly by the denominator, it is easier to follow
this rule:

| Amount | × by numerator | ÷ by denominator | = answer |

Complete the workings to find the fraction of
each amount. The first one has been done for you.

> You can draw diagrams
> to help you convert the
> top-heavy fractions into
> mixed numbers.

a $\frac{2}{3}$ of 8 km $\qquad$ $8 \times 2 = 16$ $\qquad$ $16 \div 3 = \frac{16}{3} = 5\frac{1}{3}$ km

b $\frac{3}{4}$ of 5 m $\qquad$ $5 \times 3 = \ldots\ldots$ $\qquad$ $\ldots\ldots \div 4 = \frac{}{4} = \ldots\ldots \frac{}{4}$ m

c $\frac{3}{5}$ of 9 t $\qquad$ $9 \times 3 = \ldots\ldots$ $\qquad$ $\ldots\ldots \div 5 = \frac{}{5} = \ldots\ldots \frac{}{5}$ t

d $\frac{2}{7}$ of 10 kg $\qquad$ $10 \times 2 = \ldots\ldots$ $\qquad$ $\ldots\ldots \div 7 = \frac{}{7} = \ldots\ldots \frac{}{7}$ kg

Now try Exercise 7.5 on page 77 of Coursebook 8.

7.5 Multiplying and dividing fractions

When simplifying fractions, divide the top (numerator) and bottom (denominator) of the fraction by the same number:

$$\frac{12 \div 3}{15 \div 3} = \frac{4}{5}$$

1 Draw a line linking each fraction to its correct simplified form. One has been done for you.

$\frac{2}{4}$	$\frac{1}{3}$
$\frac{3}{9}$	$\frac{2}{3}$
$\frac{4}{20}$	$\frac{1}{2}$
$\frac{6}{8}$	$\frac{4}{5}$
$\frac{4}{6}$	$\frac{1}{5}$
$\frac{12}{15}$	$\frac{3}{4}$

2 Look at this diagram. $\frac{1}{3}$ is shaded.

When you work out $\frac{1}{2}$ of $\frac{1}{3}$ you can see that the answer is $\frac{1}{6}$.

So $\frac{1}{2}$ of $\frac{1}{3} = \frac{1}{2} \times \frac{1}{3} = \frac{1 \times 1}{2 \times 3} = \frac{1}{6}$

Follow this rule to multiply fractions:

fraction × fraction = $\dfrac{\text{numerator} \times \text{numerator}}{\text{denominator} \times \text{denominator}}$ = answer

Use the rule above to work out these multiplications.

a $\dfrac{1}{2} \times \dfrac{1}{4} = \dfrac{1 \times 1}{2 \times \ldots} = \dfrac{1}{\ldots}$

b $\dfrac{1}{3} \times \dfrac{1}{4} = \dfrac{1 \times 1}{\ldots \times \ldots} = \dfrac{1}{\ldots}$

c $\dfrac{1}{3} \times \dfrac{1}{5} = \dfrac{1 \times 1}{\ldots \times \ldots} = \dfrac{1}{\ldots}$

d $\dfrac{1}{2} \times \dfrac{1}{7} = \dfrac{1 \times 1}{\ldots \times \ldots} = \dfrac{1}{\ldots}$

3 Look at these multiplications. Write whether each one is TRUE or FALSE. If the answer is false, work out the correct answer.

a $\dfrac{1}{2} \times \dfrac{1}{5} = \dfrac{1}{10}$ . . . .

b $\dfrac{1}{6} \times \dfrac{1}{4} = \dfrac{1}{10}$ . . . .

c $\dfrac{1}{6} \times \dfrac{1}{3} = \dfrac{2}{18}$ . . . .

d $\dfrac{1}{5} \times \dfrac{1}{8} = \dfrac{1}{40}$ . . . .

4 Work out the these multiplications. Write each answer in its simplest form. The first one has been done for you.

a $\dfrac{1}{2} \times \dfrac{4}{5} = \dfrac{1 \times 4}{2 \times 5} = \dfrac{4}{10}$ $\dfrac{4}{10} = \dfrac{4 \div 2}{10 \div 2} = \dfrac{2}{5}$

b $\dfrac{2}{3} \times \dfrac{1}{4} = \dfrac{2 \times 1}{\ldots \times \ldots} = \dfrac{2}{\ldots}$

c $\dfrac{3}{4} \times \dfrac{2}{5}$

d $\dfrac{3}{5} \times \dfrac{1}{6}$

Now try Exercise 7.8 on page 80 of Coursebook 8.

8 Symmetry

8.1 Classifying quadrilaterals

A quadrilateral is a 2D shape that has four straight sides. Two common examples of quadrilaterals are the square and rectangle.

1 Look at this quadrilateral.

Complete these sentences using the following numbers and words.

> cut   opposite   4   half   2

A quadrilateral has . . . . straight sides.

A diagonal is a line that joins two . . . . corners of a quadrilateral.

All quadrilaterals have . . . . diagonals.

The diagonals always . . . . (cross) each other.

Sometimes the diagonals bisect each other. Bisect means to cut in . . . .

2 Look at square ABCD.

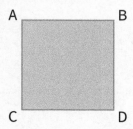

Complete these sentences using the following numbers and words:

> bisect   BD   4   length   CD   4   90

All sides are the same . . . .

AB is parallel to . . . . and AC is parallel to . . . .

All the angles are . . . . °.

It has . . . . lines of symmetry. Draw these on the diagram.

It has order . . . . rotational symmetry.

The diagonals AD and BC . . . . each other at 90°.

3   Look at rectangle EFGH.

E   F

G   H

Complete these sentences using the following numbers and words:

> EH   GH   2   opposite   2   90   FG   FH

. . . . sides are the same length.

EG is parallel to . . . . and EF is parallel to . . . .

All the angles are . . . .°.

It has . . . . lines of symmetry. Draw these on the diagram.

It has order . . . . rotational symmetry.

The diagonals . . . . and . . . . bisect each other.

4 Look at kite IJKL.

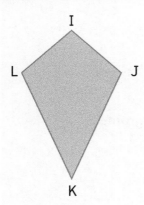

Complete these sentences using the following numbers and words:

| IL | line | equal | not | parallel | LJ | LK | 1 |

IJ is the same length as .... and JK is the same length as ....

None of the sides is ....

Angle ILK is .... to angle IJK but angle LIJ is .... equal to angle LKJ.

It has one .... of symmetry. Draw this on the diagram.

It has order .... rotational symmetry.

The diagonal IK bisects the diagonal ....

5 This question is all about parallelogram MNOP.

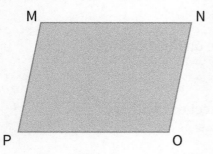

Complete these sentences using the following numbers and words:

| equal | no | bisect | MP | opposite | 2 | MN | MPO |

.... sides are the same length.

NO is parallel to .... and PO is parallel to ....

Angle PMN is .... to angle NOP and angle MNO is equal to angle ....

It has .... lines of symmetry.

It has order .... rotational symmetry.

The diagonals .... each other.

6 This question is all about rhombus QRST.

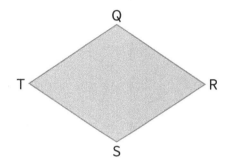

Complete these sentences using the following numbers and words:

2	parallel	TSR	all	QRS	rotational	90

.... sides are the same length.

Opposite sides are ....

Angle TQR is equal to angle .... and angle QTS is equal to angle ....

It has .... lines of symmetry. Draw them on the diagram.

It has order two .... symmetry.

The diagonals bisect each other at .... °.

Now try Exercise 8.3 on page 89 of Coursebook 8.

8.2 Drawing nets of solids

A **net** shows the 2D layout of a 3D shape. The net will fold up to make the 3D shape.

Imagine the shape is a box, then follow these steps:

Step 1: Draw the base of the box.

Step 2: Draw the sides and ends of the box.

Step 3: Draw the top of the box.

> It is easier to draw the net of a cuboid on squared paper.

1 Complete the net for each of these cuboids.

> A cuboid has six faces, so there should be six parts to each net.

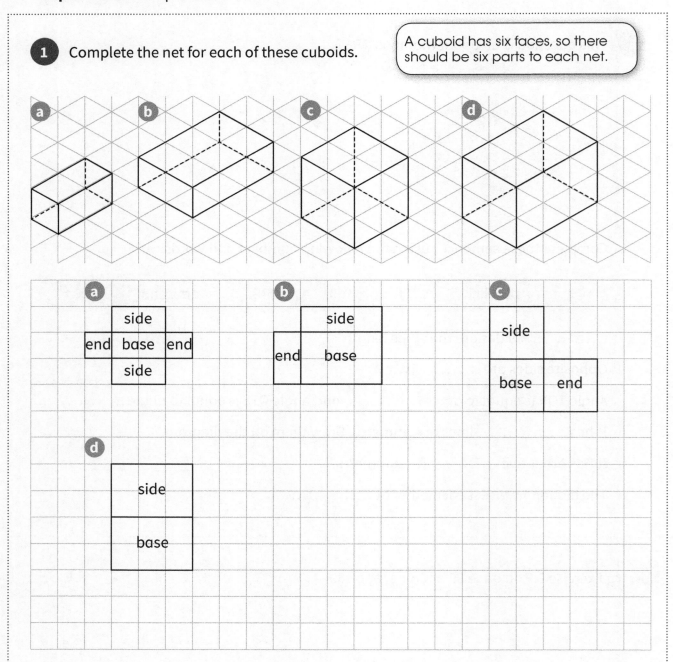

2 Complete the net for each of these pyramids.

 a

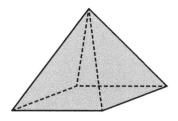

This pyramid has a square base and four identical triangular sides.

base

side

b

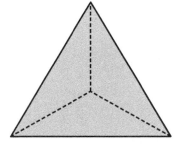

This pyramid has a triangular base and three identical triangular sides. It is easier to draw nets for this pyramid on triangular dotty paper.

side

base

Now try Exercise 8.4 on page 90 of Coursebook 8.

8.3 Making scale drawings

A scale drawing is a drawing that shows something in real life.

The scale shows the connection between the lengths on the drawing and the lengths in real life.

An example of a scale is:

> 1 cm represents 10 m

> This means that 1 cm on the drawing is worth 10 m in real life.

So, 2 cm on the drawing represents 2 × 10 = 20 m in real life, 3 cm on the drawing represents 3 × 10 = 30 m in real life, etc.

---

1 Complete the workings below using a scale of   1 cm represents 5 m

a 2 cm on the drawing represents 2 × 5 = ... m in real life.

b 3 cm on the drawing represents 3 × 5 = ... m in real life.

c 8 cm on the drawing represents . . . . . . × 5 = ... m in real life.

> To go from the drawing to real life you MULTIPLY by the scale.

2 Complete the workings below using a scale of   1 cm represents 20 cm

a 2 cm on the drawing represents 2 × 20 = ... cm in real life.

b 3 cm on the drawing represents . . . . × 20 = ... cm in real life.

c 6 cm on the drawing represents . . . . × . . . . . . = ... cm in real life.

3 Complete the workings below using a scale of   1 cm represents 10 m

a 20 m in real life represents 20 ÷ 10 = ... cm on the drawing.

b 30 m in real life represents 30 ÷ 10 = ... cm on the drawing.

c 70 m in real life represents . . . . ÷ 10 = ... cm on the drawing.

> To go to real life from the drawing, you DIVIDE by the scale.

4 Complete the workings below using a scale of [1 cm represents 50 cm]

a 100 cm in real life represents 100 ÷ 50 = ... cm on the drawing.

b 150 cm in real life represents .... ÷ 50 = ... cm on the drawing.

c 300 cm in real life represents .... ÷ .... = ... cm on the drawing.

5 Look at the cards below. The light grey cards are scale drawing measurements. The dark grey cards are real life measurements.

Draw a line to match each light grey card to the correct dark grey card.

The scale used is [1 cm represents 2 m]

One has been done for you.

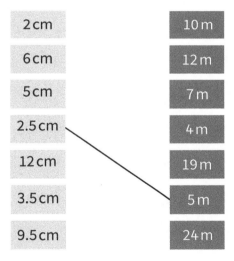

2 cm	10 m
6 cm	12 m
5 cm	7 m
2.5 cm	4 m
12 cm	19 m
3.5 cm	5 m
9.5 cm	24 m

Now try Exercise 8.5 on page 92 of Coursebook 8.

9.1 Collecting like terms

Like terms are terms that contain the same letter.

You **simplify** an expression by **collecting like terms**.

Expressions should be written following a few simple rules. Here are some examples:

Write $3x$ not $3 \times x$ Write $x + y$ not $y + x$

Write $3x$ not $x3$ Write xy not yx

Write $3x + 2$ not $2 + 3x$ Write $1 - 2x$ not $-2x + 1$

---

1 Draw a line to join each rectangular card to its matching oval card.
The first one has been done for you.

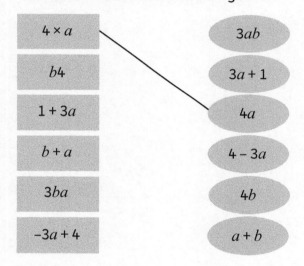

2 Look at the statements below. Three are true and three are false.

Write TRUE or FALSE next to each one. If a statement is false, write the correct answer.

a $x + 2x = 3x$ ....

b $4y - y = 4$ ....

c $7z + 3z = 10z$ ....

d $2a + 2a + a = 5a$ ....

e $4b + 3b + 2b = 10b$ ....

f $7c - 5c + c = 2c$ ....

3   Look at the following expressions. Some of them can be simplified and some cannot.

If they can be simplified, put a tick next to them and work out the simplified answer. If they cannot be simplified, mark them with a cross. The first two have been done for you.

a $4a + 12a$ ✓ $16a$ **b** $4a + 7b$ ✗

c $2b + b$ ....   **d** $8e - e$ ....

e $4c - 2d$ ....   **f** $9f + 2$ ....

4   Each of these expressions simplifies to $3x$ or $-3x$. Draw a line joining each rectangular card to the correct simplified oval card. The first one has been done for you.

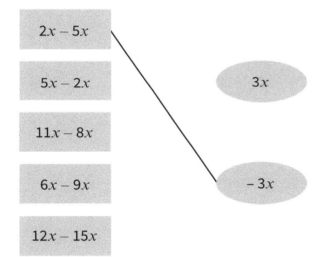

$2x - 5x$

$5x - 2x$

$3x$

$11x - 8x$

$6x - 9x$

$-3x$

$12x - 15x$

5   Look at the statements below. Three are true and three are false.

Write TRUE or FALSE next to each one.
If a statement is false, write the correct answer.

> You can only simplify when the letters are the same.

a $7b - 2b + b = 6b$ ....   **b** $8c - 4c - c = 2c$ ....

c $6h - 5h + 4 = h + 4$ ....   **d** $9k - 2k + 2m + 4m = 7k + 7m$ ....

e $9p - p + 4 - 1 = 11p$ ....   **f** $10 - 5 + 3v - 6v = 5 - 3v$ ....

Now try Exercise 9.1 on page 97 of Coursebook 8.

9.2 Expanding brackets

You can use a box method to multiply numbers, like this:

$3 \times 14 = 3 \times (10 + 4)$

×	10	4
3	30	12

$3 \times 14 = 30 + 12 = 42$

> $3 \times (10 + 4)$ can be written as $3(10 + 4)$

> You use the table to **expand** the bracket $3(10 + 4)$ to get $3 \times 10 + 3 \times 4$

---

1 Complete the boxes to work out the answers.

a 4×18

×	10	8
4		

$4 \times 18 = \ldots\ldots + \ldots\ldots = \ldots\ldots$

b 3×21

×	20	1
3		

$3 \times 21 = \ldots\ldots + \ldots\ldots = \ldots\ldots$

2 Complete the boxes to show two different ways to multiply 6 by 58.

a $6 \times 58 = 6 \times (50 + 8)$

×	50	8
6		

$6 \times 58 = \ldots\ldots + \ldots\ldots = \ldots\ldots$

b $6 \times 58 = 6 \times (60 - 2)$

×	60	−2
6		

$6 \times 58 = \ldots\ldots - \ldots\ldots = \ldots\ldots$

> Your answers to a) and b) should be the same.

3 Complete the boxes to simplify these expressions. Some have been started for you.

a $3(x + 5)$

×	x	5
3	$3x$	

$3(x + 5) = 3x + \ldots\ldots$

b $2(x + 9)$

×	x	9
2		

$2(x + 9) = \ldots\ldots + \ldots\ldots$

c $5(y - 1)$

×	y	−1
5		−5

$5(y - 1) = \ldots\ldots - 5$

d $4(y - 8)$

×	y	−8
4		

$4(y - 8) = \ldots\ldots - \ldots\ldots$

4 Complete the boxes to simplify these expressions. Some have been started for you.

a $3(2x + 1)$

×	$2x$	1
3	$6x$	

$3(2x + 1) = 6x + \ldots\ldots$

b $5(4x + 9)$

×	$4x$	9
5		

$5(4x + 9) = \ldots\ldots + \ldots\ldots$

c $2(3y - 7)$

×	$3y$	−7
2		−14

$2(3y - 7) = \ldots\ldots - 14$

d $5(8y - 5)$

×	$8y$	−5
5		

$5(8y - 5) = \ldots\ldots - \ldots\ldots$

Now try Exercise 9.2 on page 98 of Coursebook 8.

9.3 Constructing and solving equations

You can use a flow chart like this to solve an equation.

Solve: $3x + 5 = 17$ x [× 3]   [+ 5]   17

So $x = 4$ 4   [÷ 3]   12   [− 5]   17

> Reverse the flow chart to work out the value of x.

---

1 Complete these flow charts to work out the value of x.

a $2x + 1 = 11$ x [× 2]   [+ 1]   11

$x = \ldots\ldots$ $\ldots\ldots$ [÷ 2]   10   [− 1]   11

b $5x − 2 = 18$ x [× 5]   [− 2]   18

$x = \ldots\ldots$ $\ldots\ldots$ [÷ 5] $\ldots\ldots$ [+ 2]   18

c $3(x + 4) = 21$

> Multiply out the bracket first.

$3x + 12 = 21$ x [× 3]   [+ 12]   21

$x = \ldots\ldots$ $\ldots\ldots$ [÷ 3] $\ldots\ldots$ [− 12]   21

d $4(x − 1) = 24$

$\ldots\ldots − 4 = 24$ x [× $\ldots\ldots$]   [− 4]   24

$x = \ldots\ldots$ $\ldots\ldots$ [÷ $\ldots\ldots$] $\ldots\ldots$ [+ 4]   24

2 The diagram shows a rectangle.

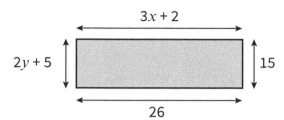

Complete the workings to find the values of x and y.

$3x + 2 = 26$ x $\boxed{\times 3}$ $\boxed{+ 2}$ 26

$x = \ldots\ldots$ $\ldots\ldots$ $\boxed{\div 3}$ $\ldots\ldots$ $\boxed{- 2}$ 26

> The lengths of the rectangle are the same, so $3x + 2 = 26$

$2y + 5 = 15$ y $\boxed{\times 2}$ $\boxed{+ 5}$ 15

$y = \ldots\ldots$ $\ldots\ldots$ $\boxed{\div 2}$ $\ldots\ldots$ $\boxed{- 5}$ 15

> The widths of the rectangle are the same, so $2y + 5 = 15$

3 This diagram shows a different rectangle.

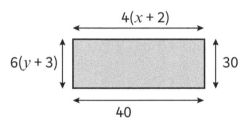

Complete the workings to find the values of x and y.

Multiply out the brackets first: $4(x + 2) = 4x + \ldots$.

$4x + \ldots = 40$ x $\boxed{\times 4}$ $\boxed{+ \ldots\ldots}$ 40

$x = \ldots\ldots$ $\ldots\ldots$ $\boxed{\div 4}$ $\ldots\ldots$ $\boxed{- \ldots\ldots}$ 40

> The lengths of the rectangle are the same, so $4(x + 2) = 40$

Multiply out the brackets first: $6(y + 3) = 6y + \ldots$.

$6y + \ldots = 30$ y $\boxed{\times 6}$ $\boxed{+ \ldots\ldots}$ 30

$y = \ldots\ldots$ $\ldots\ldots$ $\boxed{\div 6}$ $\ldots\ldots$ $\boxed{- \ldots\ldots}$ 30

> The widths of the rectangle are the same, so $6(y + 3) = 30$

Sometimes you may have to solve an equation that has the same letter on both sides of the '=' sign.

Example: $5x + 8 = 3x + 20$

Follow this method:

Subtract $3x$ from both sides: $5x - 3x + 8 = 3x - 3x + 20$

$2x + 8 = 20$

> Subtracting $3x$ from both sides leaves no x on the right.

Then use a flow chart to solve $2x + 8 = 20$.

x → $\times 2$ → $+ 8$ → 20

So $x = 6$.

6 ← $\div 2$ ← 12 ← $- 8$ ← 20

4 Complete the workings to solve these equations.

a $4x + 5 = x + 17$ Subtract x from both sides: $4x - x + 5 = x - x + 17$

$3x + \ldots\ldots = \ldots\ldots$

x → $\times 3$ → $+ \ldots\ldots$ → $\ldots$

$x = \ldots\ldots$ ← $\div 3$ ← $\ldots\ldots$ ← $- \ldots\ldots$ ← $\ldots$

b $7x + 2 = 2x + 27$ Subtract $2x$ from both sides: $7x - 2x + 2 = 2x - 2x + 27$

$\ldots\ldots x + \ldots\ldots = \ldots\ldots$

x → $\times \ldots\ldots$ → $+ \ldots\ldots$ → $\ldots$

$x = \ldots\ldots$ ← $\div \ldots\ldots$ ← $\ldots\ldots$ ← $- \ldots\ldots$ ← $\ldots$

c $10x - 4 = 8x + 12$ Subtract $8x$ from both sides: $10x - 8x - 4 = 8x - 8x + 12$

$\ldots\ldots x - \ldots\ldots = \ldots\ldots$

x → $\times \ldots\ldots$ → $- \ldots\ldots$ → $\ldots$

$x = \ldots\ldots$ ← $\div \ldots\ldots$ ← $\ldots\ldots$ ← $+ \ldots\ldots$ ← $\ldots$

Now try Exercise 9.3 on page 99 of Coursebook 8.

10.1 Calculating statistics

Here are the ages of 12 children. Each dot is one child.

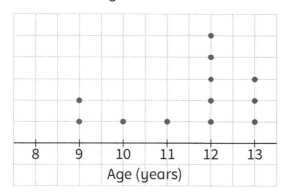

Age (years)

To find the **mean** age:

> The mean is an average.

- add up the ages

- divide by the number of children.

2 children are 9 years old	$9 \times 2 = 18$
1 child is 10 years old	$10 \times 1 = 10$
1 child is 11 years old	$11 \times 1 = 11$
5 children are 12 years old	$12 \times 5 = 60$
3 children are 13 years old	$13 \times 3 = 39$
Total	138

Mean = $138 \div 12 = 11.5$

The arrow on this diagram shows the mean.

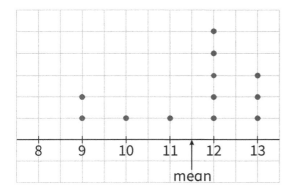

mean

> You divide by 12 because there are 12 children.

> The mean is always somewhere between the largest and smallest numbers.

1 This diagram shows the number of books that 12 students have.

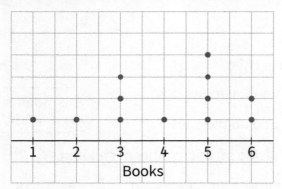

a Write down the number of students who have two books . . . .

b Complete this sentence:

. . . . . . students have 5 books. They have . . . . . . books all together.

c Work out the mean number of books. You can show your working beside the diagram, as in the example on page 73.

d Draw an arrow on the diagram to show the mean.

2 This diagram shows the scores from 20 turns of the spinner.

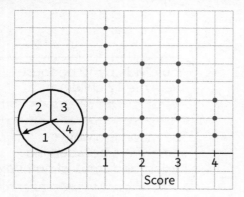

a Write down the number of times the score was 1. . . . .

b Write down the number of times the score was 4. . . . . . .

c Work out the mean score.

d Draw an arrow on the diagram to show the mean score.

3 This diagram shows the number of brothers that 14 girls have.

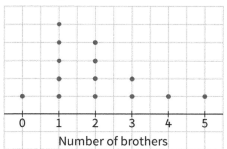

Number of brothers

a Write down the number of girls with 1 brother. . . . .

b Write down the number of girls with 4 brothers. . . . .

c Work out the mean number of brothers.

d Draw an arrow on the diagram to show the mean.

4 This diagram shows the ages of some young people.

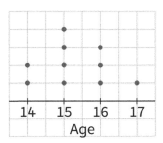

Age

a Write down the number of young people. . . . . . .

b Work out the mean age.

c Draw an arrow on the diagram to show the mean.

5 This table shows the number of days some employees were absent from work.

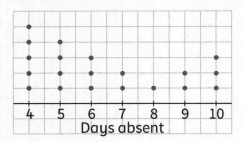

a Write down the number of employees who were absent for 10 days. . . . . . .

b Write down the total number of employees. . . . . . .

c Work out the mean number of days the employees were absent.

d Draw an arrow on the diagram to show the mean.

Here is the first diagram in this chapter again.

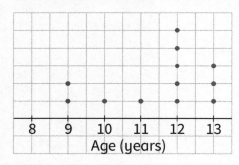

The **range** of the ages is the difference between the oldest and the youngest person.

The range is 13 – 9 = 4 years.

You can put the numbers in a frequency table like this:

Age	9	10	11	12	13
Frequency	2	1	1	5	3

Two students are 9 years old. The frequency of 9 is 2.

6 Here is the diagram from Question 1.

a What is the range? ......

b Complete this frequency table.

Books	1	2	3	4	5	6
Frequency	1		3			

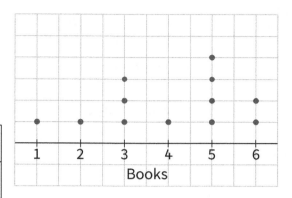

Books

7 Here is the diagram from Question 2.

a What is the range? ......

b Complete this frequency table.

Score	1	2	3	4
Frequency	7			

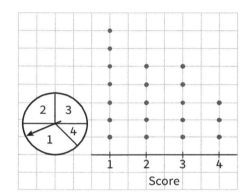

Score

8 Here is the diagram from Question 3.

a What is the range? ......

b Complete this frequency table.

Brothers	0	1				
Frequency						

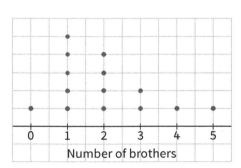

Number of brothers

9 Here is the diagram from Question 4.

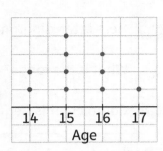

a What is the range? . . . . . .

b Complete this frequency table.

Age				
Frequency				

10 Here is the diagram from Question 5.

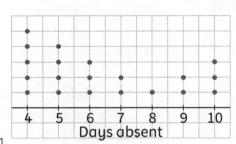

a What is the range? . . . . . .

b Complete this frequency table.

Days absent	4	5					
Frequency							

Now try Exercise 10.1 on page 103 of Coursebook 8.

10.2 Grouped data

Here are the heights, in cm, of 20 plants.

7 8 10 10 12 13 15 16 18 19 20 20 23 24 26 26 27 28 30 32

Here is a frequency table to show these heights.

Height	6–10	11–15	16–20	21–25	26–30	31–35
Frequency	4	3	5	2	5	1

The heights are in six **classes**.

The first four heights, 7 cm, 8 cm, 10 cm, 10 cm, are in the class 6–10 cm.

The next three heights, 12 cm, 13 cm, 15 cm, are in the class 11–15 cm.

1 Here are the times, in seconds, that people can hold their breath.

25 26 28 28 31 32 32 34 34 35 36 39 40 41 46 46 47 47

Put the times in the frequency table.

Time	25–29	30–34	35–39	40–44	45–49
Frequency					

2 Here are the masses, in kilograms, of some young children.

12 12 14 14 14 15 17 19 21 21 21 22 22 24 25 27 27 27 30 32 32 33

Put the masses in the frequency table.

Mass	11–15	16–20	21–25	26–30	31–35
Frequency					

3 Here are the ages of some people.

23 25 26 29 33 33 38 38 40 41 42 45 45 46 49 51 53 54 57 58 58
61 63 66

Put the ages in the frequency table.

Age	20–29	30–39	40–49	50–59	60–69
Frequency					

4 Here is a frequency table of race times, in minutes.

Time (min)	40–49	50–59	60–69	70–79	80–89	90–99
Frequency	12	32	54	38	17	5

Here are six more times: 52   55   58   72   81   84

Add these times to complete a new frequency table.

Time (min)	40–49	50–59	60–69	70–79	80–89	90–99
Frequency						

Now try Exercise 10.2 on page 105 of Coursebook 8.

11 Percentages

11.1 Calculating percentages

Remember these facts about percentages and fractions:

$50\% = \dfrac{1}{2}$ $25\% = \dfrac{1}{4}$ $10\% = \dfrac{1}{10}$

You have $84. You can work out the percentages of this amount like this:

100%	50%	25%	10%
$84	$42	$21	$8.40

42 is $\dfrac{1}{2}$ of 84 21 is $\dfrac{1}{4}$ of 84

You can use these to work out other percentages:

$5\% = \dfrac{1}{2}$ of $10\% = \dfrac{1}{2}$ of $\$8.40 = \$4.20$

$30\% = 3 \times 10\% = 3 \times \$8.40 = \$25.20$

$15\% = 25\% - 10\% = \$21 - \$8.40 = \$12.60$

---

1 A watch costs $120.

a Complete the table to show the percentages.

100%	50%	25%	10%
$120			

b Complete the calculations for the price of the watch.

i $75\% = 50\% + 25\% = \ldots\ldots\ldots$

ii $35\% = 25\% + 10\% = \ldots\ldots\ldots$

iii $12.5\% = \dfrac{1}{2}$ of $25\% = \ldots\ldots\ldots$

2 You earn $28.

a Complete the table to show the percentages.

100%	50%	25%	10%
$28			

b Complete the calculations.

i $5\% = \frac{1}{2}$ of 10% = ...

ii 20% = 2 × 10% = ...

iii 70% = 50% + 20% = ...

3 The cost of a holiday is $600.

a Complete the table to show the percentages.

100%	50%	25%	10%
$600			

b Work out the following percentages.

i 75% = ...   **ii** 35% = ...

iii 60% = ...   **iv** 12.5% = ...

4 The cost of a car is $3200.

a Find 50% of $3200 ....   **b** Find 10% of $3200 ....

c Find 20% of $3200 ....   **d** Mia says: '60% = 3 × 20%.'

Show Mia's calculation.

....

e Shen says: '60% = 50% + 10%.'

Show Shen's calculation.

....

5 A bike costs $310.

Complete the table to show the percentages.

100%	10%	20%	30%	40%
$310				

6 A laptop costs $700.

Complete the table to show the percentages.

100%	10%	20%	40%	60%	80%
$700					

7 The rent on a flat is $2800.

Complete the table to show the percentages.

100%	5%	10%	15%	20%	25%
$2800					

Now try Exercise 11.1 on page 111 of Coursebook 8.

11.2 Percentage increases and decreases

The price of a printer is $139.

10% of $139 is $13.90.

If the price **increases** by 10%, the new price is $139 + $13.90 = $152.90.

If the price **decreases** by 10%, the new price is $139 – $13.90 = $125.10.

> Add an increase; subtract a decrease.

1 The price of a guitar is $460.

a Find 10% of $460. . . . .

b If the price of the guitar is increased by 10%, what is the new price? . . . .

c If the price of the guitar is decreased by 10%, what is the new price? . . . .

2 The price of a phone is $320.

a Find 10% of $320. . . . .

b Find 5% of $320. . . . .

c If the price of the phone is increased by 5%, what is the new price? . . . .

d If the price of the phone is decreased by 5%, what is the new price? . . . .

3 The price of a coffee table is $380.

a Complete this table.

100%	50%	10%	5%
$380			

b The price of the table increases by 50%. What is the new price? . . . .

c The price of the table increases by 10%. What is the new price? . . . .

d The price of the table decreases by 5%. What is the new price? . . . .

4 The population of a town is 35 000.

a Complete this table.

100%	10%	20%	30%	40%
35 000				

b Work out the population of the town after these changes.

i Increase of 10% . . . .   **ii** Decrease of 20% . . . .

iii Increase of 30% . . . .   **iv** Decrease of 40% . . . .

5 In a sale, all prices are reduced by 10%.

Complete the table.

Item	Original price	10%	Sale price
Shirt	$25	$2.50	$22.50
Trousers	$45		
Coat	$90		
Shoes	$80		

Now try Exercise 11.2 on page 113 of Coursebook 8.

11.3 Finding percentages

Use a calculator in this section.

In a test, Raha gets 26 marks out of 40.

She changes her mark to a percentage like this:

$\frac{26}{40}$ = 26 ÷ 40 = 0.65   0.65 × 100 = 65%

This means that 26 out of 40 is the same as 65 out of 100.

> Change the fraction to a decimal by division. You can use a calculator to do this.

1 In a test, Anders gets 17 out of 20. Change this to a percentage.

....

2 In a test, Alicia gets 12 out of 30. Change this to a percentage.

....

3 In a test, Hassan gets 48 out of 60. Change this to a percentage.

....

4 In a test, Sasha gets 69 out of 75. Change this to a percentage.

....

5 Here are Oditi's marks for four subjects. Write each one as a percentage in the table.

English	13 out of 20	65%
Maths	34 out of 40	
Physics	42 out of 60	
Chemistry	52 out of 80	

6 In an election, 25 000 people voted.

a 8000 people voted for the Yellow Party.

What percentage is this? ....

b 6500 people voted for the Orange Party.

What percentage is this? ....

c 4250 people voted for the Grey Party.

What percentage is this? ....

7 There are 800 students in a college.

a 496 students are women. What percentage is this? ....

b What percentage are men? ....

8 There are 3200 people in a town.

a 896 people are under 18 years old. What percentage is this? ....

b 704 are over 60. What percentage is this? ....

Now try Exercise 11.3 on page 115 of Coursebook 8.

12.1 Drawing a perpendicular bisector

The **midpoint** of a line is the point that is exactly half way.

The **perpendicular bisector** cuts a line exactly in half at 90°.

The steps below explain how to draw the perpendicular bisector of a line.

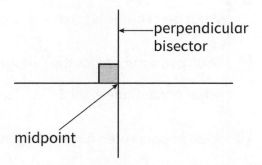

Step 1: Open your compasses to a little over half the length of the line AB. In this case AB is 7 cm, so 4 cm would be fine. Put your compass point on point B and draw a large arc.

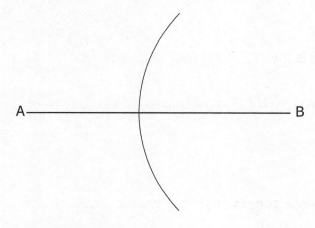

Step 2: Keep your compasses open to 4 cm. Put your compass point on point A and draw another large arc.

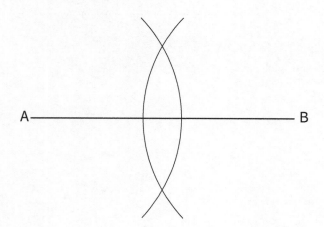

Step 3: Draw a straight line to join points where the two arcs cross.

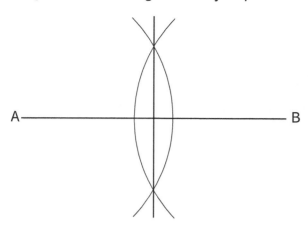

---

1 Copy the steps to draw the perpendicular bisector of the line AB.

A ———————————————————— B

Now try Exercise 12.2 on page 123 of Coursebook 8.

12.2 Drawing an angle bisector

The **angle bisector** cuts an angle exactly in half.

The steps below explain how to draw an angle bisector.

Step 1: Open your compasses, put your compass point on the dot at B and draw an arc that crosses lines AB and BC, as shown.

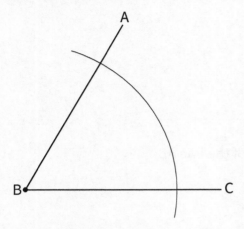

Step 2: Put your compass point on points D and E and draw equal arcs that cross in the middle of the angle.

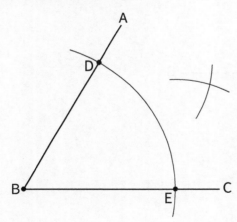

Step 3: Draw a straight line to join point B to where the two arcs cross.

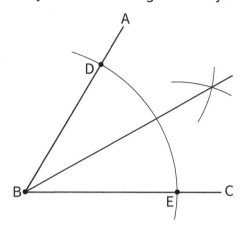

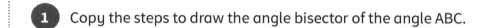

1 Copy the steps to draw the angle bisector of the angle ABC.

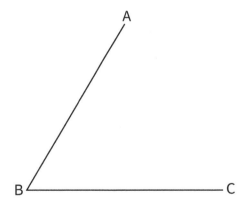

Now try Exercise 12.3 on page 124 of Coursebook 8.

12.3 Constructing triangles

You only need a ruler and a compass to draw some triangles accurately.

When you know the length of all three sides, it is called **SSS** or **Side, Side, Side**.

The following steps explain how to accurately draw triangle ABC.

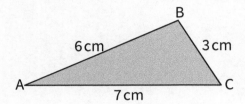

Step 1: Draw a line 7 cm long. Label it AC.

Step 2: Open your compasses to 6 cm. Put your compass point on A and draw an arc above the line AC.

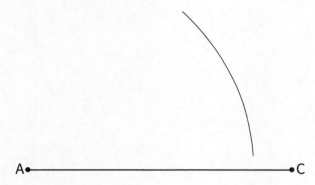

Step 3: Open your compasses to 3 cm. Put your compass point on C and draw an arc above the line AC that crosses your first arc.

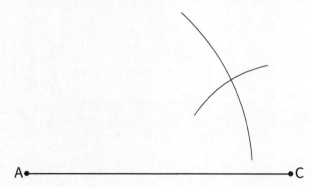

Step 4: Draw a dot where your two arcs cross and label it B. Draw straight lines from A to B and from C to B.

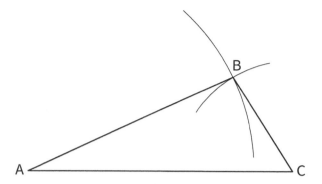

1 In the space below, copy the steps to accurately draw triangle ABC.

You can also draw a triangle using only a ruler and compasses when you know the following facts:

- that the triangle contains a right angle
- the length of the longest side (the hypotenuse)
- the length of one other side.

This is called **RHS** or **Right**, **Hypotenuse**, **Side**.

The following steps explain how to accurately draw triangle DEF.

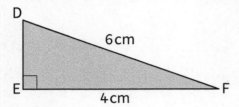

Step 1: Draw a line GF that is 8 cm long.

> This is twice as long as the 4 cm base

Step 2: Open your compasses to 6 cm, which is the same as the length of the hypotenuse, DF. Draw the perpendicular bisector of the line GF. You can now label the points D and E.

> If you're not sure how to do this, look at page 88.

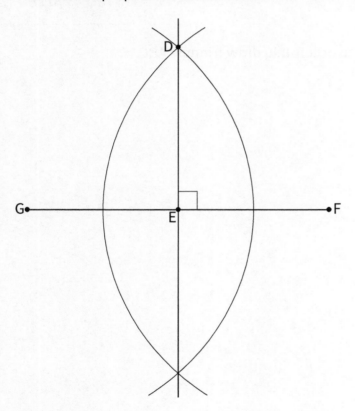

Step 3: Join point D to point F with a straight line.

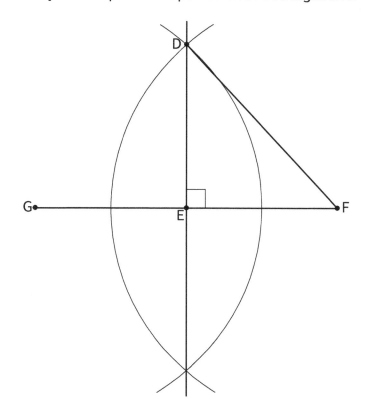

EF is now the base of your triangle and DF is the hypotenuse of your triangle.

1 In the space below, copy the steps to accurately draw triangle DEF.

Now try Exercise 12.4 on page 127 of Coursebook 8.

13 Graphs

13.1 Drawing graphs of equations

You need to be able to find positive and negative coordinates for a point on a coordinate grid.

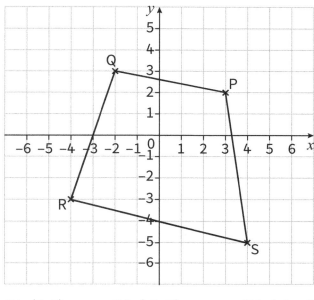

Write the x-coordinate first.

P is (3, 2)   Q is (–2, 3)   R is (–4, –3)   S is (4, –5)

1 a Write down the coordinates of the vertices of this rectangle.

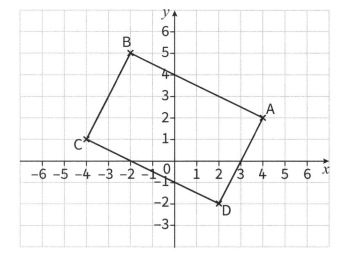

A (...... , ...)   B (...... , ...)   C (...... , ...)   D (...... , ...)

b E (–3, 3) is on one of the sides. Mark it on the grid.

c F (0, –1) is on one of the sides. Mark it on the grid.

2

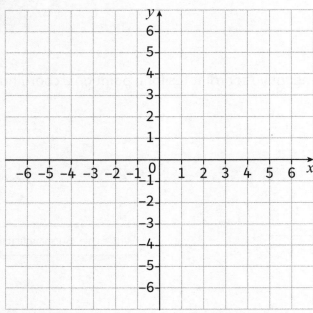

a Put these points on the grid. Mark each one with a cross (✗).

(–4, 2)   (–2, 6)   (6, 2)   (4, –2)

b Join the points to make a rectangle.

c The centre of the rectangle is (1, 2). Mark this on the grid.

Vertical and horizontal lines have equations.

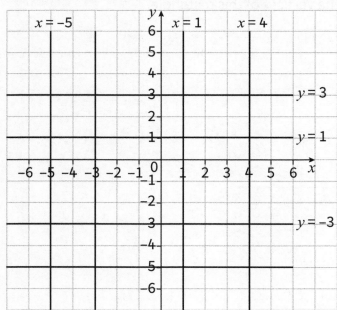

Vertical lines have the equation x = a number

Horizontal lines have the equation y = a number

3 Two of the lines on the grid shown do not have equations.

Write down the equations for these two lines. ....

4

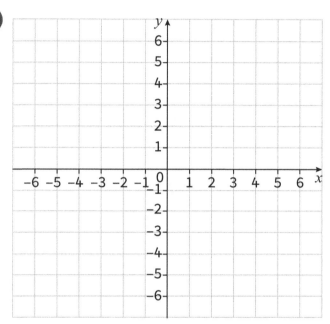

a Put these points on the grid. Mark each one with a cross (✗).

(5, –2)   (–3, –2)   (2, –2)   (–6, –2)   (0, –2)

b Draw a straight line through these points.

> If the points are not in a straight line, check that you have plotted them correctly.

c Write down the equation of the line. ....

5 **a** Put these points on the grid in Question 3. Mark each one with a cross (✗).

(3, –6)   (3, 2)   (3, 0)   (3, 5)   (3, –4)

b Draw a straight line through these points.

c Write down the equation of the line. ....

6

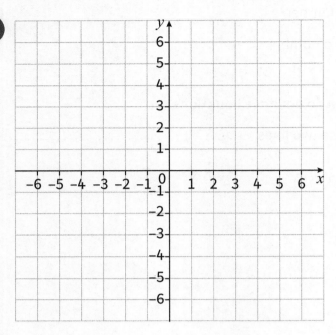

a Put these points on the grid. Mark each one with a cross (✗).

(3, –3)   (–4, 4)   (2, –2)   (–6, 6)   (1, –1)

b Draw a straight line through these points.

c Are the following points on the line? Write YES or NO for each.

i (–3, 3) . . . .

ii (4, 4) . . . .

iii (–6, –6) . . . .

iv (5, –5) . . . .

7 Here is an equation: $y = x + 2$

a Complete this mapping diagram.

x	$+2$	y	(x, y)
4	⟶	6	(4, 6)
3	⟶	......	....
2	⟶	4	(2, 4)
1	⟶	......	....
0	⟶	......	....
–1	⟶	1	(–1, 1)
–2	⟶	......	....
–3	⟶	......	....
–4	⟶	......	....

b Plot the points on this grid.

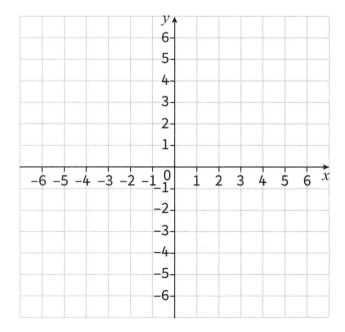

c Join the points with a straight line.

d Label the line with the equation $y = x + 2$

8 Here is an equation: $y = x - 3$

a Complete this mapping diagram.

x	-3	y	(x, y)
5	⟶	2	(5, 2)
4	⟶	......	....
3	⟶	0	(3, 0)
2	⟶	......	....
1	⟶	......	....
0	⟶	......	....
−1	⟶	......	....
−2	⟶	−5	(−2, −5)
−3	⟶	......	....

b Plot the points on this grid.

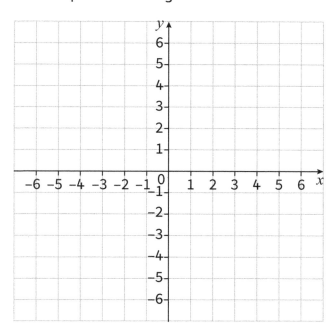

c Join the points with a straight line.

d Label the line with the equation $y = x - 3$

9 Here is an equation: $y = \frac{1}{2}x$

a Complete this mapping diagram.

x	$\div 2$	y	(x, y)
6	$\longrightarrow$	3	(6, 3)
4	$\longrightarrow$	......	....
2	$\longrightarrow$	......	....
0	$\longrightarrow$	......	....
−2	$\longrightarrow$	−1	(−2, −1)
−4	$\longrightarrow$	......	....
−6	$\longrightarrow$	......	....

b Plot the points on this grid.

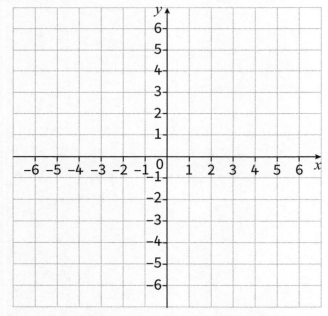

c Join the points with a straight line.

d Label the line with the equation $y = \frac{1}{2}x$

Now try Exercise 13.1 on page 131 of Coursebook 8.

13.2 The midpoint of a line segment

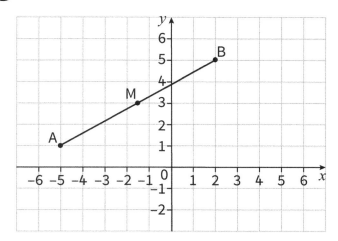

M is half way between A and B.

M is the midpoint of AB.

A is (–5, 1) and B is (2, 5). The midpoint M is (–1.5, 3)

1

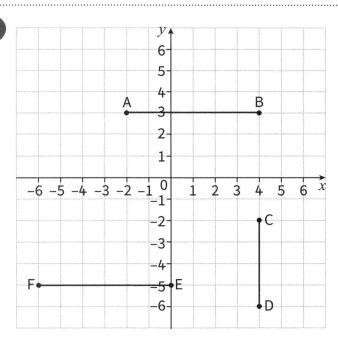

Complete the sentences.

a A is (......,......)   B is (......,......)   The midpoint of AB is (......,......)

b C is (......,......)   D is (......,......)   The midpoint of CD is (......,......)

c E is (......,......)   F is (......,......)   The midpoint of EF is (......,......)

2

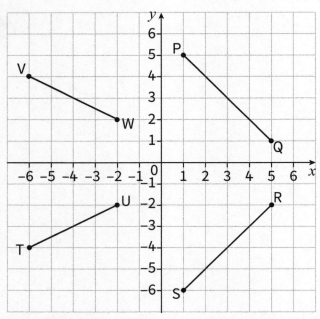

Complete the sentences.

a P is (......, ...)   Q is (......, ...)   The midpoint of PQ is (......, ...)

b R is (......, ...)   S is (......, ...)   The midpoint of RS is (......, ...)

c T is (......, ...)   U is (......, ...)   The midpoint of TU is (......, ...)

d V is (......, ...)   W is (......, ...)   The midpoint of VW is (......, ...)

Now try Exercise 13.3 on page 135 of Coursebook 8.

14 Ratio and proportion

14.1 Sharing in a ratio

This example shows how you can share an amount in a ratio between three people.

Ali, Bin and Cal share $12 in the ratio 1:2:3.

Ali	Bin	Cal	
$1	$2	$3	$1 + $2 + $3 = $6
$1	$2	$3	$1 + $2 + $3 = $6
$2	$4	$6	$2 + $4 + $6 = £12

> For every $1 Ali gets, Bin gets $2 and Cal gets $3.

So Ali gets $2, Bin gets $4 and Cal gets $6.

---

1   Dai, Eva and Fin share $16 in the ratio 1:3:4.

Complete the working to show how much they each get.

Dai	Eva	Fin	
$1	$3	$4	$1 + $3 + $4 = $8
$......	$......	$......	$...... + $...... + $...... = $......
$......	$......	$......	$...... + $...... + $...... = $16

So Dai gets $....., Eva gets $....... and Fin gets $......

2   Gan, Han and Ian share 30 counters in the ratio 2:3:5.

Complete the working to show how many counters they each get.

Gan	Han	Ian	
●●	●●●	●●●●●	2 + 3 + 5 = 10 counters
			...... + ... + ... = ... counters
			...... + ... + ... = ... counters
......	......	......	...... + ... + ... = 30 counters

So, Gan gets ...... counters, Han gets ...... counters and Ian gets ...... counters.

This is an example of a quicker method you can use to share in a ratio.

Jie, Kaj and Lin share $60 in the ratio 3 : 4 : 5. How much do they each get?

Jie	Kaj	Lin	
$3	$4	$5	3 + 4 + 5 = 12 and 60 ÷ 12 = 5
$3 × 5 = $15	$4 × 5 = $20	$5 × 5 = $25	

(Check total: $15 + $20 + $25 = $60 ✓)

3 Mo, Nik and Oli share $88 in the ratio 2 : 5 : 4. How much do they each get?

Mo	Nik	Oli	
$2	$5	$4	2 + 5 + 4 = ... and 88 ÷ ...... = ...
$2 × ...... = $......	$5 × ...... = $......	$4 × ...... = $......	

(Check total: $... + $... + $... = $.....)

4 Pat and Qiu and Ros share $100 in the ratio 7 : 8 : 5. How much do they each get?

Pat	Qiu	Ros	
$7	$8	$5	7 + 8 + 5 = ... and 100 ÷ ...... = ...
$7 × ...... = $......	$8 × ...... = $......	$5 × ...... = $......	

(Check total: $...... + $...... + $...... = $......)

Now try Exercise 14.2 on page 143 of Coursebook 8.

15 Probability

15.1 The probability that an outcome does not happen

The weather forecast says that the probability it will rain tomorrow is 20%.

Probabilities are always written as a percentage, a decimal or a fraction.

The probability of rain could be written as 20% or 0.2 or $\frac{1}{5}$.

The probability it will not rain tomorrow is 1 – the probability that it will.

The probability it will not rain is 80% or 0.8 or $\frac{4}{5}$.

---

1 Fill in the missing percentage, decimal or fraction.

a 40% + ... = 100%　　**b** 0.7 + ... = 1　　**c** $\frac{1}{3}$ + ... = 1

d 85% + ... = 100%　　**e** 0.51 + ... = 1　　**f** $\frac{3}{8}$ + ... = 1

2 Here are seven decimal number cards.

a There are three pairs that add up to 1. What are they?

.... and ....

.... and ....

.... and ....

b Which number is the odd one out? ....

3 The probability that Jake throws a 4 with a dice is $\frac{1}{6}$.

Find the probability that Jake does not throw a 4. ....

4 The probability that a plane arrives on time is 75%.

Write down the probability that it does not arrive on time. . . . .

5 The probability that Anders is late for school is $\frac{1}{20}$.

Write down the probability that he is not late. . . . .

6 The probability that Alicia wins a race is 30%.

Write down the probability that Alicia loses the race. . . . .

7 The probability that a horse wins a race is $\frac{3}{5}$.

Write down the probability that the horse does not win. . . . .

8 The probability that United will win a football match is 75%.

Ahmed says: 'The probability United will lose is 25%.'

a Is Ahmed correct? . . . .

b Give a reason for your answer.

. . . .

. . . .

Now try Exercise 15.1 on page 149 of Coursebook 8.

15.2 Equally likely outcomes

Here are eight cards. Each one has a letter.

Tanesha takes a card at random. This means each card is equally likely to be taken.

Each card has the same probability of being taken.

There are eight cards. One card has a letter A. Two cards have a letter O.

The probability of taking A is $\frac{1}{8}$.

The probability of taking an O is $\frac{2}{8}$ or $\frac{1}{4}$.

> You can simplify the fraction.

The probability of taking an A or an O is $\frac{3}{8}$.

The probability of not taking an A or an O is $\frac{5}{8}$.

---

1 Look at the cards in the example.

Write down the probability of taking:

a the letter F . . . .

b a letter L . . . .

c a letter F, O or L . . . .

2 Look at the cards in the example.

Write down the probability of:

a taking the letter T . . . . **b** not taking the letter T . . . .

c taking the letter A or B . . . . **d** not taking the letter A or B . . . .

3 Here are seven cards. Each one has a letter.

Harsha takes a card at random.

Write down the probability that the card is:

a a letter A . . . .

b the letter B . . . .

c the letter A or B . . . .

d a letter that is not A . . . .

e a letter that is not A or N . . . .

4

Shen throws a fair six-sided dice.

Find the probability that Shen throws:

> 'Fair' means that all numbers are equally likely.

a a 6 . . . .

b a 5 . . . .

c a 5 or 6 . . . .

d a number less than 5 . . . .

e an even number . . . .

5

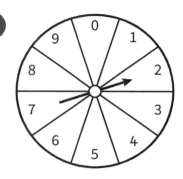

This is a fair spinner.

Xavier spins the arrow.

Find the probability that it points to:

'Fair' means the pointer has the same probability of pointing to each digit.

a the 4 . . . .

b the 7 . . . .

c the 0 . . . .

d the 4, 5 or 6 . . . .

e an odd number . . . .

Now try Exercise 15.2 on page 150 of Coursebook 8.

15.3 Listing all possible outcomes

This is a spinner. Anders spins the arrow twice.

You can show all the possible outcomes in a table.

Second spin

First spin		1	2	3	4
	1	1, 1	1, 2	1, 3	1, 4
	2	2, 1	2, 2	2, 3	2, 4
	3	3, 1	3, 2	3, 3	3, 4
	4	4, 1	4, 2	4, 3	4, 4

Find 2, 3 in the table.

2, 3 means 2 on the first spin and 3 on the second spin.

---

1 Look at the table of outcomes in the example.

a Explain what 4, 4 means.

....

....

b Explain the difference between 1, 3 and 3, 1.

....

....

c How many different outcomes are there? ....

d The outcome 1, 3 has a total of 4.

Find two other outcomes with a total of 4 ....

e Find two outcomes with a total of 7. ....

2 Jake spins a coin. Mia throws a dice.

a Complete this table of outcomes.

Dice

		1	2	3	4	5	6
Coin	**Head**	H, 1					
	Tail				T, 4		

b How many outcomes are there? ....

c List the four outcomes which include a 5 or a 6.

....

3

Maha spins both spinners.

a Complete this table of outcomes.

Second spinner

		C	D	E
First spinner	**A**	A, C		
	B			
	C			

b How many outcomes are there?..

c How many outcomes include letter C? ....

Now try Exercise 15.3 on page 152 of Coursebook 8.

16 Position and movement

16.1 Transforming shapes

When you **transform** a shape, the shape you start with is called the **object**. The shape you finish with is called the **image**.

When you **reflect** shapes you need to know the equation of the mirror line on a coordinate grid.

---

1 Write the equation of each of the mirror lines shown on the grid. Choose from the answers below. The first one has been done for you.

| $y = 1$ | $x = 5$ | ~~$y = 5$~~ | $y = 3$ | $x = 2$ |

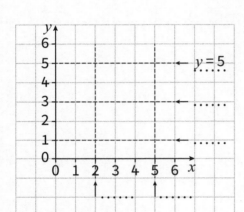

Remember that the vertical lines start $x = \ldots$ and the horizontal lines start $y = \ldots$

2 Complete each reflection in the mirror line shown.

a
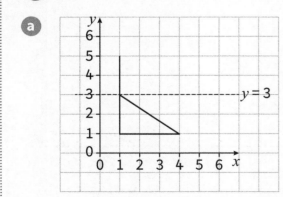

b
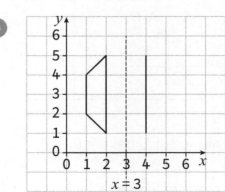

Remember to reflect each shape one corner at a time, then join the points with straight lines.

116

3 Complete each translation.

> Remember to move each shape one corner at a time.

a 3 squares right and 1 square up

b 4 squares left and 3 squares down

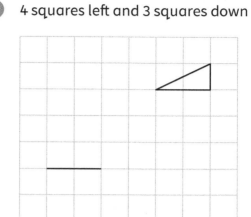

4 Rotate these shapes 90° clockwise about the centre of rotation given.

> Use tracing paper to trace the shape, then put your pencil point on the centre of rotation and turn the paper 90° clockwise.

a Centre (2, 3)

b Centre (3, 4)

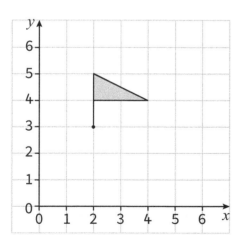

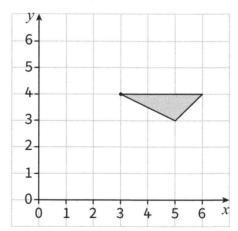

5 Rotate these shapes 180° about the centre of rotation given.

a Centre (3, 3)

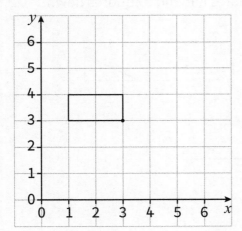

b Centre (2, 4)

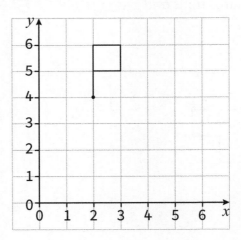

6 Rotate these shapes 90° anticlockwise about the centre of rotation given.

Use tracing paper to trace the shape, then put your pencil point on the centre of rotation and turn the paper 90° anticlockwise.

a Centre (3, 2)

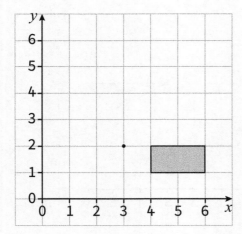

b Centre (4, 3)

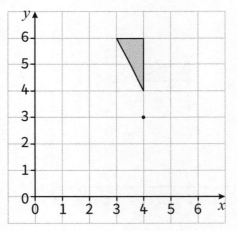

Now try Exercise 16.1 on page 159 of Coursebook 8.

16.2 Enlarging shapes

An enlargement of a shape is a copy of the shape that is either bigger or smaller than the original.

You enlarge a shape using a **scale factor** and **centre of enlargement**.

1 Complete these enlargements using a scale factor of 2 and the centre of enlargement marked C.

Follow these steps:

Step 1: Count the number of squares from the centre of enlargement to the nearest corner of the rectangle. Multiply this number by 2 to find the new distance from the centre of enlargement. Plot this point.

Step 2: Count the length and width, in squares, of the rectangle. Multiply both of these by 2 to find the new length and width. Draw the enlarged rectangle from the corner you have already plotted.

a

b

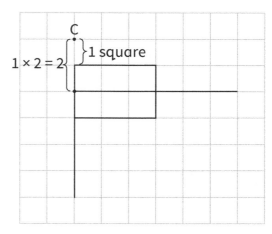

c

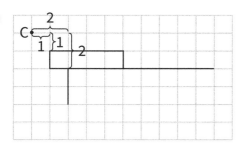

2 Complete these enlargements using a scale factor of 3 and the centre of enlargement given.

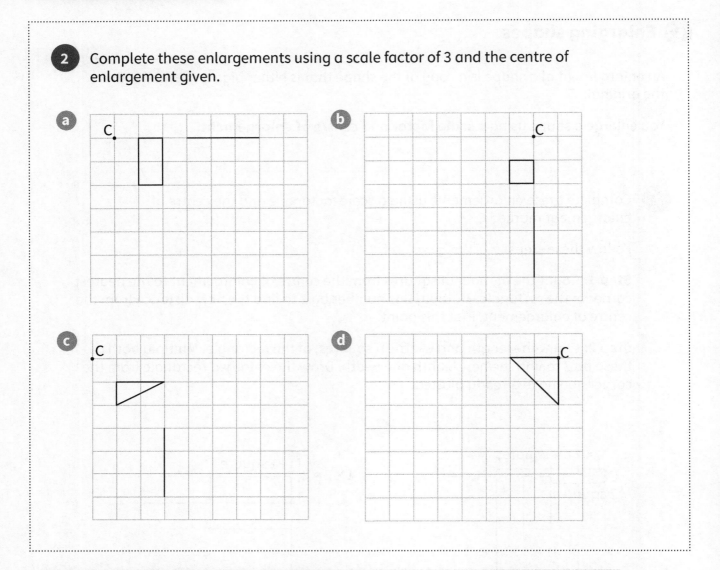

Now try Exercise 16.2 on page 162 of Coursebook 8.

17.1 The area of a triangle

This rectangle and triangle are drawn on centimetre squared paper.
Each square has an area of $1\,cm^2$.

The area of the rectangle $= base \times height$

$= 4 \times 2$

$= 8\,cm^2$

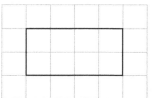

The area of the triangle $= \frac{1}{2} \times$ the area of the rectangle

$= \frac{1}{2} \times 8$

$= 4\,cm^2$

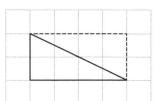

---

1 Complete the workings to find the areas of these rectangles and triangles.

a Area of rectangle $= base \times height$

$= 3 \times \ldots\ldots = \ldots\ldots\ cm^2$

Area of triangle $= \frac{1}{2} \times$ area of rectangle

$= \frac{1}{2} \times \ldots\ldots = \ldots\ldots\ cm^2$

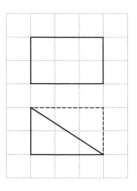

b Area of rectangle $= base \times height$

$= 4 \times \ldots\ldots = \ldots\ldots\ cm^2$

Area of triangle $= \frac{1}{2} \times$ area of rectangle

$= \frac{1}{2} \times \ldots\ldots = \ldots\ldots\ cm^2$

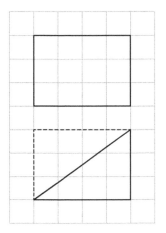

c Area of rectangle = base × height

= 5 × ...... = ... cm^2

Area of triangle = $\frac{1}{2}$ × area of rectangle

= $\frac{1}{2}$ × ...... = ... cm^2

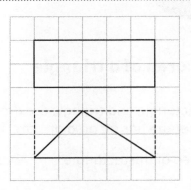

2 Draw a line linking each triangle to its correct area. The first one has been done for you.

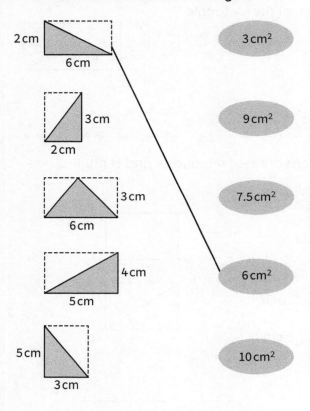

2 cm / 6 cm

3 cm^2

3 cm / 2 cm

9 cm^2

3 cm / 6 cm

7.5 cm^2

4 cm / 5 cm

6 cm^2

5 cm / 3 cm

10 cm^2

Now try Exercise 17.1 on page 166 of Coursebook 8.

17.2 The areas of a parallelogram and trapezium

You can work out the area of a parallelogram by making the parallelogram into a rectangle like this:

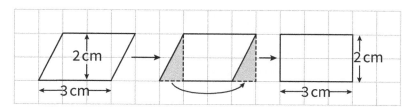

Area = base × height = 3 × 2 = 6 cm²

---

1 Work out the area of these parallelograms by making them into rectangles.

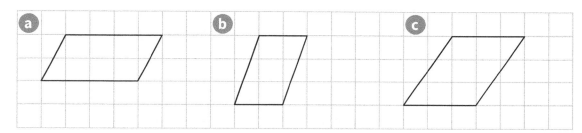

a	b	c
Area = base × height	Area = base × height	Area = base × height
= 4 ×	= 2 ×	= . . . . . . × . . . . . .
= . . . . . . cm²	= . . . . . . cm²	= . . . . . . cm²

You can work out the area of a trapezium in three steps like this:

Step 1: top + bottom

Step 2: step 1 ÷ 2

Step 3: step 2 × height

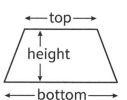

e.g. 3 + 5 = 8

8 ÷ 2 = 4

4 × 6 = 24

area = 24 cm²

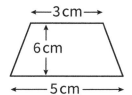

2   Complete the workings to find the area of these trapeziums.

a   **Step 1:** $4 + 6 = 10$

        Step 2: $10 \div 2 = 5$

        Step 3: $5 \times 3 = \ldots\ldots$ cm^2

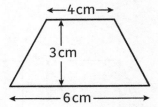

b   **Step 1:** $5 + \ldots\ldots = \ldots\ldots$

        Step 2: $\ldots\ldots \div 2 = \ldots\ldots$

        Step 3: $\ldots\ldots \times 6 = \ldots\ldots$ cm^2

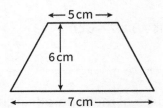

c   **Step 1:** $\ldots\ldots + \ldots\ldots = \ldots\ldots$

        Step 2: $\ldots\ldots \div 2 = \ldots\ldots$

        Step 3: $\ldots\ldots \times \ldots\ldots = \ldots\ldots$ cm^2

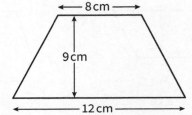

Now try Exercise 17.2 on page 168 of Coursebook 8.

17.3 The area and circumference of a circle

The circumference of a circle is the distance around the edge of it. The circumference is the special name for the perimeter of a circle.

1 Label the parts of the circles shown. Use all the words below.

area   diameter   circumference   radius

 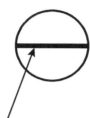  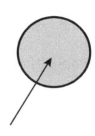

....

You can work out the circumference of a circle using this formula:

Circumference = π × diameter   or $C = π × d$

The value you can use for π is 3.14.

2 Complete the workings to find the circumference of each circle.

a
5 cm

$d = 5\,cm$

$C = π × d = 3.14 × 5$

$= ......\ cm$

b
4 cm

$d = 4\,cm$

$C = π × d = 3.14 × ......$

$= ......\ cm$

c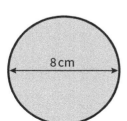
8 cm

$d = ...\ cm$

$C = π × d = 3.14 × ......$

$= ......\ cm$

3 Complete the working to find the circumference of this circle.

Radius, $r = 3$ cm

Diameter, $d = 2 \times 3 = $ ...... cm

$C = \pi \times d = 3.14 \times$ ...... $=$ ...... cm

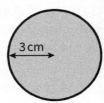

3 cm

> Remember that the diameter is twice the radius.

You can work out the area of a circle using this formula:

Area = $\pi \times$ radius^2 or $A = \pi \times r^2$

4 Complete the workings to find the area of these circles.

 a

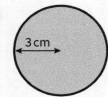

3 cm

$r = 3$ cm

$A = \pi \times r^2 = 3.14 \times 3^2$

$= 3.14 \times 9$

$=$ ...... cm^2

b

2 cm

$r = 2$ cm

$A = \pi \times r^2 = 3.14 \times 2^2$

$= 3.14 \times$ ......

$=$ ...... cm^2

c

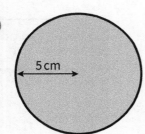

5 cm

$r = $ ...... cm

$A = \pi \times r^2 = 3.14 \times$ ......^{2}

$= 3.14 \times$ ......

$=$ ...... cm^2

5 Complete the working to find the area of this circle.

Diameter, $d = 8$ cm

Radius, $r = 8 \div 2 = $ ...... cm

$A = \pi \times r^2 = 3.14 \times$ ......^{2}

$= 3.14 \times$ ...... $=$ ...... cm^2

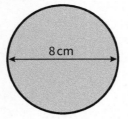

8 cm

> Remember that the radius is half the diameter.

Now try Exercise 17.3 on page 170 of Coursebook 8.

17.4 The areas of compound shapes

A **compound shape** is made from simple shapes such as rectangles, triangles, parallelograms, etc.

1 Complete the workings to find the area of these shapes.

a

4 cm

6 cm

Area = base × height

= 6 × 4

= . . . . . . cm²

b

4 cm

6 cm

Area = $\frac{1}{2}$ × base × height

= $\frac{1}{2}$ × 6 × 4

= $\frac{1}{2}$ × . . . . . .

= . . . . . . cm²

c

5 cm

6 cm

Area = base × height

= 6 × . . . . . .

= . . . . . . cm²

2 These compound shapes are made from the shapes in Question 1.

Use your answers to Question 1 to find the area of these compound shapes.

a

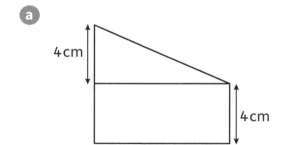

4 cm

4 cm

6 cm

Area = rectangle + triangle

= . . . . . . + ...

= . . . . . . cm²

b

5 cm

4 cm

6 cm

Area = rectangle + parallelogram

= . . . . . . + ...

= . . . . . . cm²

c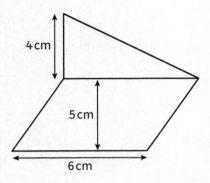

Area = parallelogram + triangle

= ...... + ...

= ...... cm^2

3 **a** This compound shape is made from two rectangles, A and B.

Work out the missing lengths.

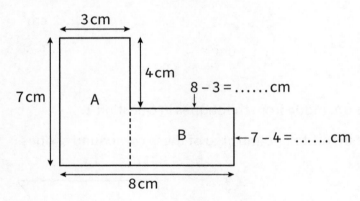

b Complete the workings to find the area of the compound shape.

Area A = base × height   Area B = base × height

$\quad$ = 3 × ...... $\quad$ = 5 × ......

$\quad$ = ... cm^2 $\quad$ = ... cm^2

Total area = Area A + Area B = ... + ... = ... cm^2

Now try Exercise 17.4 on page 171 of Coursebook 8.

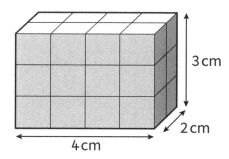

17.5 The volumes and surface areas of cuboids

You can work out the volume of a cuboid like this:

Number of cubes on top layer = 4 × 2 = 8

Number of layers = 3

Volume of cuboid = 8 × 3 = 24 cm³

This is the same as using the formula:

Volume = length × width × height or V = l × w × h

---

 1 Work out the volume of these cuboids.

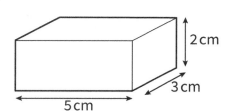

a

V = l × w × h

= 5 × 3 × 2

= ...... cm³

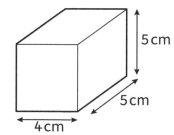

b

V = l × w × h

= ...... × ...... × ......

= ...... cm³

 c

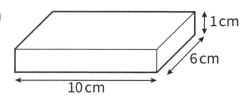

V = l × w × h

= ...... × ...... × ......

= ...... cm³

2 Draw a line linking these cuboids to their correct volumes.

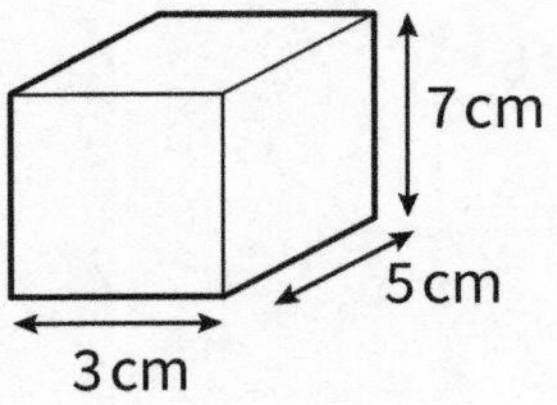

7 cm
5 cm
3 cm

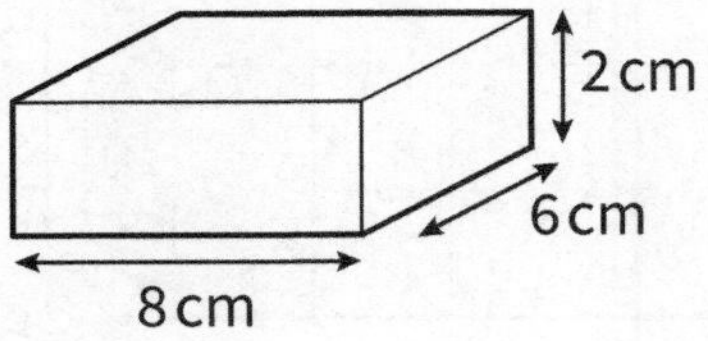

2 cm
6 cm
8 cm

140 cm^3

105 cm^3

144 cm^3

96 cm^3

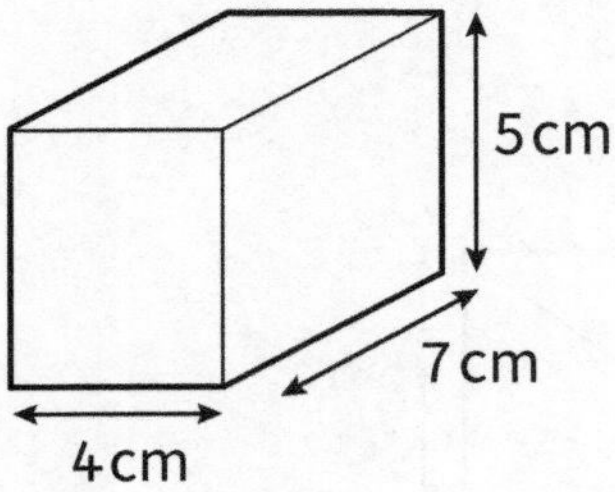

5 cm
7 cm
4 cm

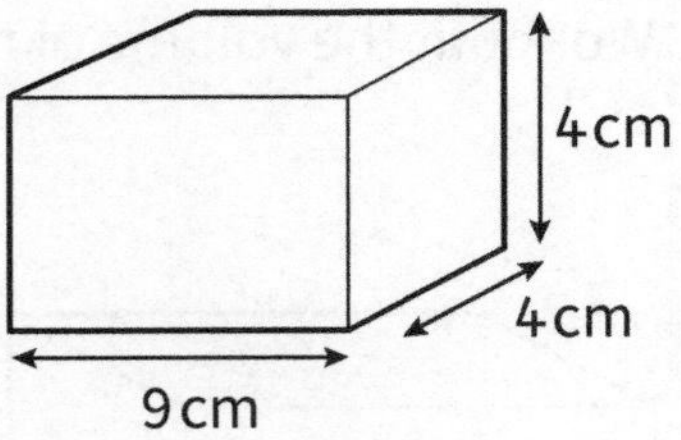

4 cm
4 cm
9 cm

3 Work out the volume of this cuboid.

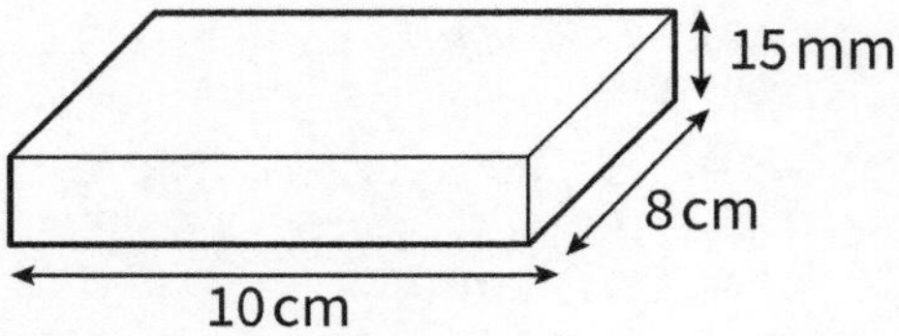

15 mm
8 cm
10 cm

The length and width are given in cm, but the height is in mm. Start by converting the height to cm, then use the formula as normal.

....

....

....

....

The surface area of a cuboid is the total area of ALL its faces.

Follow these steps to work out the surface area of a cuboid:

Step 1: Make a sketch of every face of the cuboid and write on the length and width.

Step 2: Work out the area of every face – write it in the centre of the face.

Step 3: Add together all the areas.

Make sure you have worked out the area of all SIX faces.

4 Complete the workings to find the surface area of these cuboids.

a

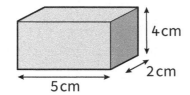

4 cm

2 cm

5 cm

front face | 20 cm² | 4 cm
5 cm

back face | ...... cm² | 4 cm
5 cm

top face | 10 cm² | 2 cm
5 cm

bottom face | ...... cm² | ...... cm
5 cm

left end face | ...... cm² | 4 cm
2 cm

right end face | ...... cm² | ...... cm
...... cm

Total surface area = 20 + ... + 10 + ... + ... + ... = ... cm²

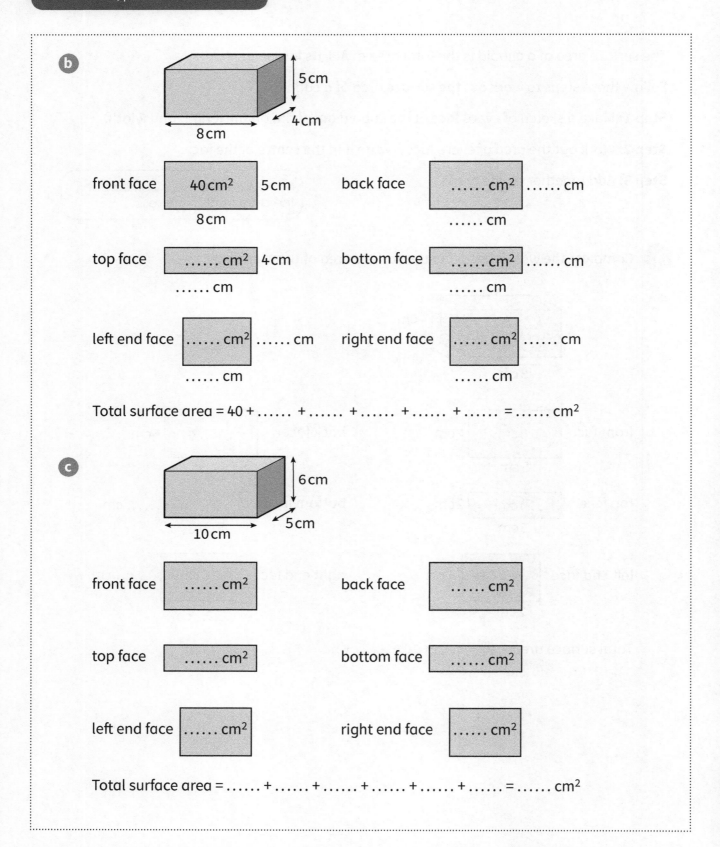

b

front face | 40 cm² | 5 cm   back face | ...... cm² | ...... cm
8 cm   ...... cm

top face | ...... cm² | 4 cm   bottom face | ...... cm² | ...... cm
...... cm   ...... cm

left end face | ...... cm² | ...... cm   right end face | ...... cm² | ...... cm
...... cm   ...... cm

Total surface area = 40 + ... + ... + ... + ... + ... = ... cm²

c

front face | ...... cm²   back face | ...... cm²

top face | ...... cm²   bottom face | ...... cm²

left end face | ...... cm²   right end face | ...... cm²

Total surface area = ... + ... + ... + ... + ... + ... = ... cm²

Now try Exercise 17.5 on page 173 of Coursebook 8.

17.6 Using nets of solids to work out surface areas

You can work out the surfce area of any solid shape by following these steps.

Step 1: Sketch a net of the shape and write the dimensions onto the net.

Step 2: Work out the area of each face.

Step 3: Work out the total area of all the faces.

1 Complete the workings to find the surface area of each of these solid shapes.

a

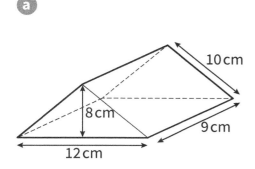
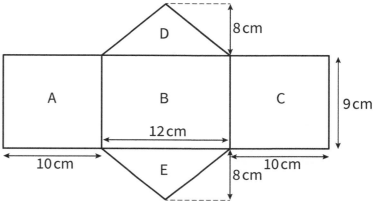

Area A = 10 × 9 = ... cm^2

Area B = 12 × 9 = ... cm^2

Area C = Area A = ... cm^2

Total area = ... + ... + ... + ... + ... = ... cm^2

Area D = $\frac{1}{2}$ × 12 × 8 = ... cm^2

Area E = Area D = ... cm^2

b

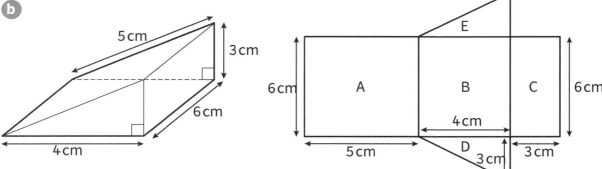

Area A = 5 × 6 = ... cm^2

Area B = 4 × ...... = ... cm^2

Area C = ... × ...... = ... cm^2

Total area = ... + ... + ... + ... + ... = ... cm^2

Area D = $\frac{1}{2}$ × 4 × 3 = ... cm^2

Area E = Area D = ... cm^2

c Look at this square-based pyramid.

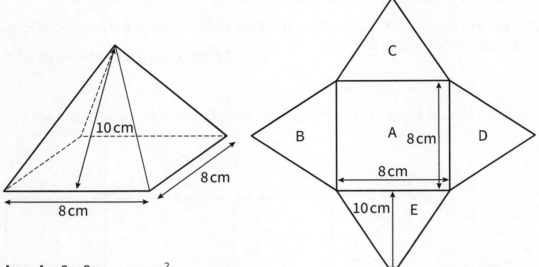

Area A = 8 × 8 = ... cm²

Area B = $\frac{1}{2}$ × 8 × 10 = ... cm²

Area of all four triangles = 4 × ...... = ... cm²

Total area = ... + ... = ... cm²

> B, C, D and E are all identical triangles, so their areas are the same.

Now try Exercise 17.6 on page 175 of Coursebook 8.

18.1 Interpreting and drawing pie charts

1 This table shows the favourite type of music of some students.

Favourite music	Dance	Electronic	Hip hop	R&B
Number of students	4	6	18	12

Complete the workings and the pie chart below.

Total number of students = 4 + 6 + 18 + 12 = ...

Number of degrees per student = 360° ÷ ...... = ...°

Number of degrees for Dance = 4 × ...... = ... °

Number of degrees for Electronic = 6 × ...... = ...°

Number of degrees for Hip hop = 18 × ...... = ...°

Number of degrees for R&B = 12 × ...... = ...°

> Check that the degrees for the four dance sections add up to 360°.

Favourite music

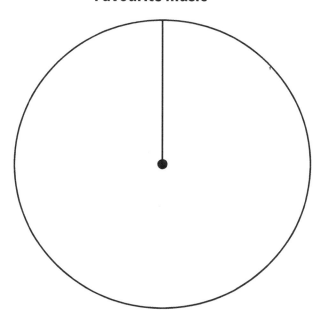

2 The pie chart shows the favourite African animal of 45 students.

a Which animal was the most popular?

....

Favourite African animal

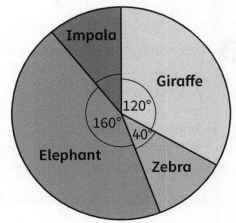

b Work out the number of degrees for the Impala section.

....

....

c Complete the workings to write the fraction of students who chose each animal. Write each fraction in its simplest form.

Giraffe: $\frac{120}{360} = \frac{1}{3}$ Zebra: $\frac{40}{360} = \frac{1}{}$ Elephant: $\frac{160}{360} = \frac{4}{}$ Impala: $\frac{}{360} = \frac{1}{}$

d Complete the workings to find the number of students who chose each animal.

> Remember: to find a fraction of an amount, divide the amount by the denominator, then multiply the answer by the numerator.

Giraffe: $\frac{1}{3} \times 45 =$ ....

....

Zebra: $\frac{1}{} \times 45 =$ ....

....

Elephant: $\frac{4}{} \times 45 =$ ....

....

Impala: $\frac{1}{} \times 45 =$ ....

....

3 The pie chart shows the favourite marine
animal of 72 students.

Favourite marine animal

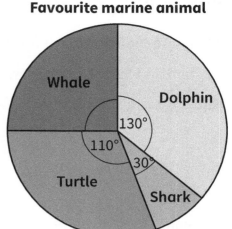

a Work out the number of degrees for the
Whale section.

....

....

b Complete the workings to write the fraction
of students wh chose each animal. Write each fraction in its simplest form.

Dolphin: $\frac{130}{360} = \frac{13}{36}$ Shark: $\frac{30}{360} = \frac{1}{}$ Turtle: $\frac{110}{360} = \frac{11}{}$ Whale: $\frac{}{360} = \frac{1}{}$

c Complete the workings to find the number of students who chose each animal.

Dolphin: $\frac{13}{36} \times 72 =$ ....

....

Shark: $\frac{1}{} \times 72 =$ ....

....

Turtle: $\frac{11}{} \times 72 =$ ....

....

Whale: $\frac{1}{} \times 72 =$ ....

....

Now try Exercise 18.2 on page 183 of Coursebook 8.

18.2 Interpreting and drawing stem-and-leaf diagrams

A **stem-and-leaf diagram** is a way of showing data in order of size.

This stem-and-leaf diagram shows the heights of 10 plants.

Key: 2 | 4 means 24 cm

2	4	7	7	8	9	9
3	0	1	5	6		

The heights of the 10 plants from smallest to largest are:

24 cm, 27 cm, 27 cm, 28 cm, 29 cm, 29 cm, 30 cm, 31 cm, 35 cm, 36 cm

---

1   This stem-and-leaf diagram shows the time, in seconds, it takes 10 students to complete a puzzle.

Key: 3 | 0 means 30 seconds

3	0	8	9	9		
4	2	4	6	7	7	8

Write the times in order of size, from the fastest to the slowest.

....

2   This stem-and-leaf diagram shows the temperature, in °C, each day Fin was on holiday.

Key: 1 | 6 means 16 °C

1	6	7	8	9
2	0	2	2	

a   Write the temperatures in order of size, from the coldest to the warmest.

....

b What is the:

i   mode   ....

ii median ....

iii range   ....

> Remember, the mode is the most common value, the median is the middle value and the range is the difference between the highest and the lowest values.

3 This stem-and-leaf diagram shows the ages of the players in a football team.

Key: 1 | 8 means 18 years

1	8	9	9			
2	0	1	2	5	6	9
3	2	5				

a Write the ages in order of size, from the youngest to the oldest.

....

b What is the:

i   mode   ....

ii median ....

iii range   ....

Now try Exercise 18.4 on page 186 of Coursebook 8.

Glossary

alternate angles angles between two parallel lines and a transversal that are in opposite positions; they make a Z-shape

angle bisector a line drawn through an angle from its vertex, dividing it into two equal parts

centre of enlargement the fixed point of an enlargement

class a group in a set of continuous data

collecting like terms gathering, by addition and subtraction, all like terms

compound shape a shape made from simpler shapes

corresponding angles angles that are in the same relative position in two or more similar or congruent shapes

decrease make or become smaller or fewer in number

enlargement a transformation that increases the size of a shape to produce a mathematically similar image

equation two different mathematical expressions, both having the same value, separated by an equals sign (=); also a way of labelling a straight line on a grid

expand multiply all parts of the expression inside the brackets by the term alongside the brackets

factor a whole number that will divide into another whole number without a remainder; 6 and 8 are factors of 24

formula (plural formulae) an equation that shows the relationship between two or more quantities

frequency table a table that lists the number of times a specific value or item occurs in a set of data (its frequency)

function machine a diagram that shows the steps in a function

highest common factor (HCF) the largest number that is a factor of two or more numbers

image a shape after a transformation

improper fraction a fraction in which the numerator is larger than the denominator

increase make or become larger or greater in number

input a number to be acted upon by a function

integer a number from the set of whole numbers: ..., −3, −2, −1, 0, 1, 2, 3, ...

lowest common multiple (LCM) the smallest possible common multiple of two numbers; 24 is the lowest common multiple of 6 and 8

mean an average of a set of numbers, found by adding all the numbers and dividing the total by how many numbers there are in the set

midpoint the centre point of a line segment

net a flat diagram that can be folded to form the faces of a solid

***n*th term** the general term of a sequence; using algebra to write the position-to-term

object a shape before a transformation

output the result after a number has been acted upon by a function

perpendicular bisector a line drawn at 90° to a line segment, dividing it into two equal parts

position-to-term rule the rule that allows any term in a sequence to be calculated, given its position number

prime number a number with exactly two factors, 1 and itself; 7, 13 and 41 are primes

range the difference between the largest and smallest number in a set

reflect transform a shape, producing the mirror image of that shape

right angle, hypotenuse, side (RHS) condition that construction of a right-angled triangle is possible, given the lengths of the hypotenuse and one other side

rule where n represents the position number of the term

scale factor the ratio by which a length is increased (or decreased)

side, side, side (SSS) condition that construction of a triangle is possible, given the lengths of all three sides

simplify divide all parts of the ratio (or fraction) by a common factor

term-to-term rule the rule to find a term of a sequence, given the previous term

transform to move a shape by reflection, rotation or translation; change a shape by enlargement